REBEL RIVERS

A Guide to
Civil War Sites
on the Potomac,
Rappahannock,
York, and James

Mark Nesbitt

STACKPOLE
BOOKS

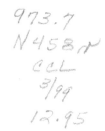
Copyright © 1993 by Mark Nesbitt

Published by
STACKPOLE BOOKS
5067 Ritter Road
Mechanicsburg, PA 17055

Cover photo by Mark Nesbitt
Cover design by Caroline Miller

All photos by the author except that of the Onondaga *(page 135), which is from the U.S. Army Military History Institute, Carlisle, PA.*

New maps by Chris Jung. Map of Ball's Bluff and line art from Battles and Leaders of the Civil War. *All other maps from the* Atlas to Accompany the Official Records of the War of the Rebellion.

Printed in the United States of America

First Edition

10 9 8 7 6 5 4 3 2 1

Library of Congress Cataloging-in-Publication Data

Nesbitt, Mark
    Rebel Rivers : a guide to Civil War sites on the Potomac, Rappahannock, York, and James / Mark Nesbitt.—1st ed.
        p.   cm.
    Includes bibliographical references and index.
    ISBN 0-8117-2538-3
    1. United States — History — Civil War, 1861–1865 — Battlefields—Guidebooks. 2. Historic sites — Potomac River Valley — Guidebooks.   3. Historic sites — Virginia — Rappahannock River Valley — Guidebooks.   4. Historic sites — Virginia — York River Valley — Guidebooks.   5. Historic sites — Virginia — James River Valley — Guidebooks.   6. Potomac River Valley — Guidebooks. 7. Rappahannock River Valley (Va.) — Guidebooks.   8. York River Valley (Va.) — Guidebooks. 9. James River Valley (Va.) — Guidebooks.   I. Title.
E641.N49   1993
973.7′09755—dc20
                                                                    93-20180
                                                                        CIP

CONTENTS

Acknowledgments vii

Introduction 1

The Upper Potomac River 9

The Chesapeake & Ohio Canal 11

Fort Frederick 12

McCoy's Ferry 13

Williamsport 14

Falling Waters 15

Shepherdstown 17

Antietam 19

Boteler's Ford 21

Harpers Ferry 22

White's Ford 24

White's Ferry 26

Ball's Bluff 27

Harrison's Island 29

Edward's Ferry 30

The Lower Potomac River 33

Arlington 33

Alexandria 35

Mount Vernon 36

Aquia Creek 38

Belle Plain 39

Fort Washington 41

Point Lookout 43

Cruising the Potomac 45

The Rappahannock River 49

Kelly's Ford on the Upper Rappahannock 50

Germanna Ford on the Rapidan 52

Ely's Ford on the Rapidan 53

Fredericksburg: 1862 54

Port Royal 59

Urbanna on the Lower Rappahannock: 1862 61

The York River 65

Gloucester Point 65

Yorktown 68

White House on the Pamunkey 71

The James River: 1862 77

Fort Monroe: 1861–1862 79

Hampton Roads: The Battle of the Ironclads 82

Norfolk 86

Portsmouth 89

Newport News 90

The Peninsula Campaign: March to May 1862 91

Drewry's Bluff 94

James River Plantations 96

The Peninsula Campaign: June to August 1862 97

Harrison's Landing 98

Traveling the James 103

The James River: 1864 107

Bermuda Hundred 109

Grant Crosses the James 113

Flowerdew Hundred 115

City Point 119

Deep Bottom 125

Aiken's Landing 128

Fort Harrison 129

Fort Brady 131

Trent's Reach, Battery Dantzler, and the
Dutch Gap Canal 132

The *Onondaga* Fiasco 134

The Confederate Capital 139

Richmond 140

Conclusion 145

Appendixes

A. Suggested Tours 149

B. Visitors' Information 155

Bibliography 160

Index 163

ACKNOWLEDGMENTS

MANY OF THOSE responsible for helping with this book are people I haven't met face-to-face. They are the hundreds of individuals who researched and answered my inquiries and sent pamphlets, brochures, and information. To these unsung heroes I extend my heartfelt appreciation.

I am especially thankful for the help of several close friends whose assistance was necessary for the writing of this book.

I am indebted to James "Seamus" Garrahy, who allowed me to be first mate on his boat for two summers in order to rehone my seamanship skills, then served as first mate on my boat as I researched the waterways in this book. I thank him for sharing his seamanship and expertise in coastal navigation. He has since started a "boat and breakfast" business on the Chesapeake Bay, sailing out of Kent Island, which sounds like a great way to see some of the historic rivers mentioned in this book.

I also want to mention the work of my friend, William A. Frassanito, who, in my opinion, is the premier historian of our generation. Bill virtually single-handedly created photohistoriography. His studies and interpretations have made us look again—even harder—at those haunting images of battlefields. He has brought them into the present that we might learn from them.

Bill discovered that many of the photos of the dead at Gettysburg were mislabeled; he corrected the problem in his first book, *Gettysburg: A Journey in Time*. In *Antietam: The Photographic Legacy of America's Bloodiest Day*, he gave names to the bloated faces of the dead and lives to the human beings that lie under the crude wooden headboards in the photographs. For *Grant & Lee: The Virginia Campaigns*, he located many obscure sites on the James River and numerous other sites relevant to the photographic history of the war's final campaigns. His published works were essential in my locating some of the sites by land on the banks of the James.

I also must thank Angela Carbone, who as a student at Gettysburg College helped in the marketing research during the conceptual stages of the book; Kim Blocher, my longtime friend, and Thom Marti, who both helped with the travel and research for sites on the Potomac and Rappahannock rivers; and Eileen Normile, now hard at work with the Kansas City Chiefs football organization, who was a fine second mate on an excursion up the Potomac.

Mary Suggs, my first editor at Stackpole, persevered through numerous changes in the concept of this book and broke them all to me gently enough to keep me writing. She has moved on to another publisher now, and I wish her the best. Ann Wagoner and Sylvia Frank, still at Stackpole, worked patiently with me on this book. I am fortunate to have William C. Davis as an editor. I have always admired his work and now have the opportunity to work with him. I also want to thank Dick Frank of Stackpole Books for his hard work on my last book, *35 Days to Gettysburg*. Writing a book is pretty much a waste of time if nobody sees it, buys it, and reads it. That's where people like Dick Frank come in. I hope I'll get to work with him on this one as well.

Jim Blankenship, historian at City Point Unit, Petersburg National Battlefield, was extremely helpful during my visit there. Dean Thomas of Thomas Publications (my "other" publisher), also a fine Civil War historian, shared his knowledge. Penny Pfohl, another longtime friend, has helped me get around Richmond and environs during several of my projects.

Some of the professionals in the tourist industry who assisted me are Sandra Mottner, Evelynton Plantation; Sarah L. Barley, coordinator, Southern Maryland Studies Center; Benjamin H. Trask, reference librarian, the Mariner's Museum, Newport News, Virginia; and Deborah Wakefield, media and community relations manager of Norfolk by the Sea at the Norfolk Convention and Visitors Bureau.

Gail Taylor, Bob Wharton, and Karen Shriver of the Flowerdew Hundred Foundation were exceedingly kind and sent me up-to-date information on the history and archaeology of the plantation. Carolyn Parsons of the Virginia State Library was helpful in tracking down historical publications. James Haskett, chief historian at Colonial National Historical Park, provided information on Yorktown and the earthworks at Gloucester Point, and Agnes Mullins of Arlington House shared some of her vast knowledge of the site and the era.

Rosemarie Martin of Culpeper, Virginia, was my contact in my research concerning Kelly's Ford on the Rappahannock, and a conversation with her led me to Mr. B. Mitchell and Dr. John T. Dailey. Kelly's Ford is right in their backyards, and through work over the years they have discovered things about the historic areas around Culpeper for the sheer love of history. They are my favorite kind of historians.

The staff at Hood College Library in Frederick, Maryland, was helpful in locating rare illustrations. And I must thank my friends on the staff at Gettysburg College Library—David Hedrick, Peggy Steinour, Susan Roach, and Frances Playfoot—for their help with this book, the last book, and throughout my many years of research.

And finally, I'd like to thank Danette Taylor for her patience and encouragement while I was writing. She is a great teacher.

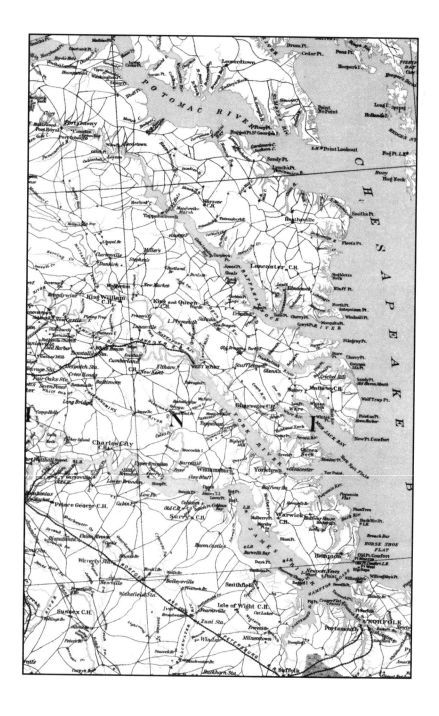

INTRODUCTION

THE RIVERS OF the eastern United States were their busiest during the American Civil War—living arteries for supply, rearmament, and reinforcement of the combatants. In addition, they and their numerous tributaries served as obstructions, causeways, impediments, and defensive bulwarks for the armies, dictating not only battle tactics but the strategy of much of the war as well.

The navigable sections of the rivers were major supply routes. The ships upon them were able to haul more ammunition, weapons, medical supplies, and foodstuffs than any wagon train and were less vulnerable to mounted raiders, the most pervasive destroyers of supplies traveling overland. Because so much of the Civil War was fought in Virginia, the rivers cutting across those battlefields—the Potomac, the Rappahannock, the York, and the James—became of paramount importance. Tiny port villages on these rivers grew to busy cities overnight as army engineers built or rebuilt railroads, corduroyed dirt roads, and constructed warehouses and barracks that the army filled with locomotives, wagons, artillery, supplies, and replacement troops.

The rivers served the Union cause better than they did the Confederate. Almost from the beginning—and dating at least from the excellent showing in battle on March 9, 1862, of the Union ironclad USS *Monitor*—the Federal Navy was able to control the major rivers in the East. Their ability to transport supplies to various ports and railheads along those rivers gave the Union commanders a tremendous edge in the art of logistics.

In the two major Confederate invasions of the North—the Antietam Campaign and the Gettysburg Campaign—Gen. Robert E. Lee chose the overland route, miles west of the navigable sections of the rivers, counting on the land to supply his troops. Using these routes and relying on the farmers in the areas to supply his invading army was a mistake, however. His first invasion started late in the growing season and ended in Sharpsburg, Maryland, before he ever got into the rich Pennsylvania croplands. His second invasion was undertaken during the third summer of the war, after the two armies already had eaten the poor farmers in the area nearly out of sustenance. In addition, once his troops ventured far enough away from their main bases of supply in and near the Shenandoah Valley, they were on their own and had to carry their military supplies with them. Once their ammunition, weapons, and equipment were depleted, there was no way to secure more.

The Confederates' fixation on the Shenandoah Valley as supplier for their army continued until the end of the war; by then the Union troops had made the valley so barren that, as one Union officer said, "a crow flying over it would have to carry his provisions." It wasn't until he was trapped in Petersburg that Lee was forced to look south, to Danville and the railroad there, for supply. Perhaps this focus on the valley was because of the Southerners' way of looking at the land as provider.

In Lee's defense, he may have been forced to rely on the Shenandoah Valley because, fairly early in the war, the Confederates had been forced to give up the great rivers in the East to the Union Navy. Those rivers—the Potomac, Rappahannock, York, and James—could have been used to transport supplies not just from "blockade runners" (which would not have been enough to sustain the Confederacy anyway) but between supply bases within the Confederacy itself. The control of those rivers could have opened the upper Confederacy to the long growing seasons in virtually every state in the South. At least during the first two years of war, when the Union blockade existed only on paper in Washington, the supplies could have come from rivers and ports throughout the Confederacy.

Breaking the blockade wasn't necessary for the Confederacy, however, at least for the first few years of war. But controlling the rivers was. Even more important was denying control of the rivers to the Union forces. If the Confederates had denied the Federals use of the Potomac, Rappahannock, York, and James by bottling them up, they would have forced the Union commanders to take the same inland route that proved unsuccessful for the Confederates.

It seems that the general who had the most success on his invasions—Ulysses S. Grant—had learned his lessons well from having had to deal with the Tennessee and Mississippi rivers in the West. Grant combined his natural tenacity with the knowledge that replacement troops from the North were nearly limitless. And his understanding of the importance of rivers for virtually mountains of supplies to his troops gave him what Lee never had: all the time and the military matériel he needed. His river-supplied invasion of the South was the one that eventually led to victory.

Earlier Union commanding generals also worked the major rivers to their advantage in devising tactics and major war strategies. In the spring of 1862, for example, Maj. Gen. George B. McClellan organized perhaps the most massive amphibious landing force in history to that date, debarking close to 100,000 troops at Fort Monroe on the Virginia Peninsula. He used the York and James rivers to supply this large force for almost three months. Then after his defeats in the Seven Days Battles, he used the rivers to extricate his forces under the cover of some of the largest artillery pieces used in the Civil War—mounted on gunboats.

It has always been my opinion that the best way to see Civil War battlefields is the same way the soldiers saw them: on foot, or perhaps on horseback. You could get the same viewpoint by bicycle, and even an automobile would work as long as you got out and walked as much as possible around the fields where men of courage marched, fought, bled, and died. The terrain—which helps determine tactics—always looks different from the soldier's point of view.

The best part about living in this age of the automobile is that many of us, especially in the East, are within easy reach of some of the major Civil War battlefields. Anyone who wishes to start at Gettysburg may visit Antietam, Harpers Ferry, and Manassas in a day. Fredericksburg, Spotsylvania, Chancellorsville, and the Wilderness can be done the next day, and Richmond and the multitude of battlefields and sites surrounding it and Petersburg are just three and a half hours away from Gettysburg.

Douglas Southall Freeman, the great historian for the South of a preceding generation, did much of his research in a library. It is doubtful that he had the opportunity to visit Gettysburg frequently, since in the 1930s it was at least a day's journey from Virginia where he wrote. And while none can fault most of his works for their chronicling of the actions of the heroes of the South and its great Army of Northern Virginia, still his readers miss something if they do not take his pages out into the sunlight and tramp the same earth his heroes once trod.

We who live in the age of the automobile have a great opportunity—a great but rapidly disappearing opportunity—as condominiums and apartment complexes, bypasses and shopping malls, parking lots and schools now cover the ground where human blood once rained. Hence the fundamental theme in my books thus far: Go to these hallowed places. Touch the earth where heroes fell. Put your feet where they charged, struggled, or lay down to bleed. See the terrain from eye level. Walk the roads and fields and hills they once walked. Feel the burning in your lungs as you ascend Little Round Top at Gettysburg, or the claustrophobia of moving through a head-high cornfield at Antietam knowing death lies somewhere just ahead. See from the field of Pickett's Charge that it is not as flat as it seems from either side or as some writers would have you believe. Stumble and slip a few times as you rapidly descend the slope at Ball's Bluff, only to find the broad, deep Potomac in the way of any escape from an enemy behind and above.

With this book as your guide, you can drive to these sites or, better yet, boat across the waters where monstrous fleets of sailing ships and ironclad vessels threw tons of shot and shell onto the land, supplied the soldiers with millions of tons of food and ammunition, and transported their broken bodies to hospitals in Washington.

This book is meant to be a historical guide, not necessarily a tour guide. It will get you to the Civil War areas and give you a detailed account of why each spot on the river was important. Many of the sites, such as Belle Plain on the Potomac or Wilcox's Landing and Weyanoke Point on the James, once among the busiest ports or river crossings in the world, are now abandoned, privately owned, or—worse yet—developed for condominiums or other short-sighted abominations that will make a lot of money for a few but steal forever the heritage of millions.

For the most part, I have given only general directions for access to these sites. A standard road map will help you find the main roads to a site, and local road signs and historical markers will take you the rest of the way. National and State Park Service employees are always helpful in answering questions. And some of the most enlightened and helpful local historians can be found behind the counter of many an old country store in Virginia.

My intention in Appendix A is not to design a site-by-site tour but to provide you with enough information to plan your own Civil War tour. Take a car with a couple of bikes to the Chesapeake & Ohio Canal and pedal to some of the fords and ferries mentioned. Take a boat for a weekend, pick up some charts, and see some of these sites from the water, the way thousands of excited, frightened young soldiers saw them for the first—and sometimes the last—time in their lives.

Most important, get to these places as soon as you can in order to see them the way they were. The same automobile that enables us to visit more Civil War battlefields than those born before us also brings the ability to commute and encourages developers to despoil battle sites. Were these sites once held sacred only because they were out of the way? This modern mobility is a blessing, a curse, and a punishment, too, as we may be seeing these sites for the last time without even realizing it. A bulldozer works that quickly. Development along riverbanks is sometimes slower than at other places, however, because of a river's unpredictability. Find these Civil War sites while they still exist, and enjoy these most important touchstones along America's Civil War rivers.

The rivers dealt with herein and their tributaries, especially around Fredericksburg and south of Richmond, drained away much American blood. They were the cleansing agents of American soil stained with that blood, as well as the agents of ablution of the "American soul," once damned by the evil of human bondage. Each one flows today still, clearer but not yet completely clean, waiting, like a Jordan of the New World, for a rebaptism of the American spirit.

REBEL RIVERS

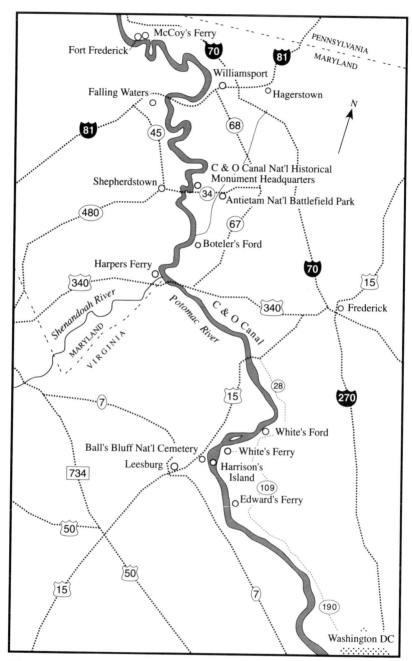

The Upper Potomac River

✦ THE UPPER ✦ POTOMAC RIVER

NAVIGABLE TO THE gates of Washington, D.C., and running between the Confederate state of Virginia and the border state of Maryland, the Potomac River served both as a buffer zone between Washington and enemy territory and as a potentially dangerous avenue for attack on the Capital of the United States by the Confederate Navy.

The importance of the Potomac River to the defense of the Union—as a natural pathway for an invading amphibious force, as an international supply route from other countries to the North, and as a waterway by which to launch Federal waterborne invasions into the South—is reflected in part by the fact that the largest Union Army, the Army of the Potomac, was named after it to show exactly where its theater of operations would be.

Virginia seceded from the Union on May 23, 1861, and suddenly enemies were within artillery range of one another just across the Potomac River. That night Union troops, most of whom had never seen a battlefield before, crossed the Long Bridge to occupy Arlington Heights in Virginia, overlooking the Potomac. Alexandria, Virginia, was occupied the next day, and both sides lost their first martyrs to the cause.

Twenty-four-year-old Union colonel Elmer Ellsworth of the Fire Zouaves, personal friend of Abraham Lincoln, saw a Confederate flag flying from the Marshall House in Alexandria. He and two others rushed to the roof of the building to pull down the Rebel banner. Coming down the stairs, he was killed by a shotgun blast from hotel keeper James Jackson. Jackson was immediately shot and bayoneted by Ellsworth's companions and died next to Ellsworth on the stairway.

Partisan newspapers on each side proclaimed their own native-born a martyr, and sectional passions rose even higher.

As U.S. warships began the blockading of major Southern ports by May 1861, Federal ships shelled Confederate batteries at Aquia Creek, Virginia, on the Potomac. A Union amphibious operation at Mathias Point on the river was repulsed in June, and Northern commanders began to plan joint operations between the army and the navy. But more important, it became evident to both sides that the Potomac and its tributaries would cut across a main theater of operations and affect strategies and tactics for most of the war. The names of some of the creeks and rivers emptying into the Potomac are written with fire in hundreds of regimental histories—Bull Run, Antietam Creek, Monocacy, Cedar Run, Aquia Creek, the Occoquan—and myriad battles and skirmishes took place up and down the Shenandoah River, which empties into the Potomac at Harpers Ferry, and the Chesapeake & Ohio Canal, across which the armies tramped practically incessantly. Battles were fought along the Potomac shores both where ships could sail and where they could not.

Perhaps it is best for touring purposes to divide the Civil War sites on the Potomac into those above the Great Falls of the Potomac and those below. First dealt with are the sites above Great Falls that can be explored by automobile, bicycle, or possibly small watercraft, such as a canoe. Guided raft trips down the Shenandoah and down the Potomac starting from above Harpers Ferry are also available (see *Appendix B*).

THE CHESAPEAKE & OHIO CANAL

THE CHESAPEAKE & OHIO (C & O) Canal was the dream of George Washington, who wanted to link the vast Chesapeake Bay, gateway to European trade, with the unsettled lands to the west via the Potomac River. The name for the canal was argued over, but the vision of connecting the Chesapeake Bay with the Ohio River, although never realized, was strong enough to lead the canal to be christened for the Chesapeake and Ohio River dream.

Construction of the canal began in 1828. It starts in Georgetown, roughly parallels the Potomac River for 184.5 miles, and ends in Cumberland, Maryland. Though the canal itself falls short of Washington's proposed link with the Ohio River, by the time the canal reached Cumberland in 1850, railroads and wagon roads from Cumberland—things never dreamed of by Wash-

THE C & O CANAL PARALLELS the course of the Potomac on the east bank for 184.5 miles, and the towpath is accessible from numerous small country roads and almost all of the main bridges crossing the Potomac from Georgetown to Cumberland. The National Park Service's Visitor Center on Route 34 across from Shepherdstown has informational pamphlets showing access points. Their address is Chesapeake and Ohio Canal National Historical Park, Ferry Hill House, Box 4, Sharpsburg, MD 21782.

ington—took cargo and passengers the remaining distance to way stations west.

The canal experienced its heyday in the 1870s, but it was doomed by the invention of the locomotive and the

☛ **WHAT · TO · SEE** Today, since it is marked at every mile, the canal can be used to find the numerous obscure fords, "ferries," and abandoned sites of pontoon bridges that were once the main crossing points of the Union and Confederate armies as they bisected the upper Potomac on invasions of enemy territory. The canal towpath mile markers start from Georgetown. The locks are numbered, so it is easy for a visitor to pinpoint the various crossings on the river by walking or bicycling on the towpath, seeing the historic sites from the perspective of the soldiers.[1]

proliferation of the railway system. Never truly a financial success, the C & O Canal was eventually abandoned as a major source of commercial transportation in 1924. It is now maintained and administered by the National Park Service. In some places only dry traces of the canal can be seen, and there are stone and iron remnants of the large locks that lowered or raised the boats in accordance with the demands of the terrain. Miraculously, the flat towpath still exists over virtually the entire length of the old canal basin and hosts hikers, campers, and bicyclists (but not motorized vehicles) throughout the outdoor seasons. Many sites of Civil War importance are accessible by the canal.

Because of its proximity to the Potomac River for nearly 185 miles, every time one of the two antagonistic armies crossed the river, they crossed the canal as well. The Union Army used portions of the canal for transport of military matériel, and the Confederate cavalry often raided across the canal, sometimes draining sections of it or bombarding dams on the Potomac. ▪

FORT FREDERICK

FORT FREDERICK WAS BUILT IN THE mid-1750s to protect British interests near the Potomac during the French and Indian War. During the Civil War, it was occupied by Union troops in order to secure both the railroad and the C & O Canal from Confederate raiders. ▪

FORT FREDERICK CAN BE reached from the canal near mile 112.4 or by automobile from Maryland Route 56.

☛ W H A T · T O · S E E   The old fort has been restored and is the occasional encampment site for reenactors of both the French and Indian War and the Civil War periods.

McCOY'S FERRY

THOUGH THE MCCOY'S FERRY CROSS-ing area was guarded by Union troops on the Maryland side, through the morning autumn mist that hung heavy on the Potomac on October 10, 1862, came Confederate troopers, dismounted, wading across the Potomac and making no splashes in the flowing water. A few dull pistol shots and the Union pickets were driven, and the main column came pounding across the Potomac with artillery wheels splashing the water high.

On up the canal a warning was given to the Union commander at old Fort Frederick, but with his small force, there was little he could do that would not be foolish against a force he estimated at 2,500 troopers with artillery. In reality, Confederate Maj. Gen. James Ewell Brown ("Jeb") Stuart had only 1,800 men, but the force no doubt looked much greater to the surprised Union commander through the early morning fog.

MCCOY'S FERRY, NOT QUITE halfway between mile mark-ers 110 and 111 on the C & O Canal, is where Jeb Stuart's cavalry crossed on October 10, 1862, at the beginning of his Chambersburg Raid. Access is from Maryland Route 56 to McCoy's Ferry Road.

Moving swiftly with a number of diversions, Jeb Stuart over the next two days rode once again around the entire Union Army commanded by Maj. Gen. George B. McClellan.[2] McClellan must have been getting tired of this: Stuart had ridden around him earlier in the year on the Virginia Peninsula. Lincoln certainly was get-ting tired of it. In a reference to a child's game called "Three times around and out," he said to his cabinet that if Stuart got around McClellan a third time, "Little Mac" would be the one out—out of the job as commander of the Army of the Potomac. ∎

WHAT · TO · SEE At the site of McCoy's Ferry is a Maryland state recreational area with picnic tables, rest rooms, a boat ramp, and a primitive campground that is used mostly by hikers and bikers on the C & O Canal.

Gen. Robert E. Lee's troops crossed the Potomac on their way to Gettysburg at the location of this bridge in Williamsport, Maryland.

WILLIAMSPORT

THE STREETS OF WILLIAMSPORT, Maryland, felt the tramp of both armies during the four-year American Civil War as Confederates attempted to destroy the Conococheague Aqueduct, then followed Gen. Thomas J. ("Stonewall") Jackson as he moved against Harpers Ferry in September 1862. Much of Lee's army crossed here during his summer invasion of Pennsylvania in June 1863 and retreated

WILLIAMSPORT CAN BE reached by following Route 11 south from Hagerstown, Maryland, or north from Martinsburg, West Virginia. Maryland Route 68 crosses through Williamsport east to west.

from Gettysburg through Williamsport after his defeat. ▪

☞ WHAT·TO·SEE An old one-lane bridge spans the canal from Williamsport and leads to the Potomac River crossings, now a park and launch ramp for boats. The pilings it rests on are purportedly the originals to a bridge across which a portion of Lee's army passed going to and from Gettysburg.

FALLING WATERS

PERHAPS THE GREATEST BLAME HEAPED upon Union Army commander Gen. George G. Meade was that he did not pursue and destroy Lee's Army of Northern Virginia after the Battle of Gettysburg in the first week of July 1863. Pursue he did, albeit cautiously. Destroy he probably could not, and he knew it. Meade had seen Lee on the defensive before, at Antietam and Fredericksburg, and had seen what Lee's veterans could do to an army once they were entrenched. Lee's engineer's eye was never wasted once he needed to be on the defensive.

By the time Meade—held up by an aggressive and agile Southern cavalry force under Jeb Stuart—had caught up with Lee on July 12, the Confederates had entrenched north of the Potomac, which had swollen above crossing levels from recent rains. Earthworks were constructed with attention to detail as if they would be subject to a siege, some with a six-foot-wide parapet, interlocking fields of fire, inner defenses, and numerous gun emplacements. The Confederate lines extended nearly eight miles from Conococheague Creek on Lee's left to the Potomac River near Downsville. Meade held a council of war, and most of his subordinates disliked the idea of attacking. Still, Meade went out and personally observed the

THE FALLING WATERS CROSSing area can be accessed by following Maryland Route 63 south from Williamsport about 2.1 miles to Falling Waters Road on the right. From the end of Falling Waters Road extension, follow the C & O Canal on foot one-half mile downstream to the Falling Waters crossing site at mile 94.4. Some development, in the form of a private campground owned by the Potomac Fish and Game Club, continues to occur along this area of the canal, so access and parking are limited.

The village of Falling Waters, West Virginia, can be reached from Williamsport, Maryland, by crossing the Potomac on Route 11 south and following Route 11 about four miles. Immediately after the road sign for the village of Falling Waters, bear left on what appears to be the original road into town. Pull over at one of the dirt parking areas and walk toward the Potomac. The sound of rushing water will lead you to the "falling waters" under the railroad bridge.

enemy defenses, then ordered plans for a reconnaissance in force drawn up for July 14. Meade, both at the time and since, has been blamed and vilified for not attacking immediately. Most of his detractors were not there to observe Lee's well-engineered fortifications. Remember that Meade was an engineer, too, and the fact that after July 12 Lee *wanted* the Yankees to attack ought to mean something as well.

By nightfall on July 13, Confederate engineers and pioneers had completed the construction of a pontoon bridge at Falling Waters (about midway between mile markers 94 and 95 on the C & O Canal). The Potomac had dropped to a fordable level at Williamsport, and by 11:00 A.M. on July 14 all but two Confederate divisions had crossed the Potomac at Williamsport and Falling Waters. These two divisions were attacked by Federal cavalry, and many of the Confederates fought with clubbed muskets and fence rails, knocking the charging troopers from their saddles. Confederate general Pettigrew was killed in the action at Falling Waters, but the Army of Northern Virginia had escaped to fight again.[3]

Though the Confederate action here at the conclusion of the Gettysburg Campaign was named after the small town, the Confederate defensive line actually extended from Falling Waters all the way beyond Williamsport to where the Conococheague Creek empties into the Potomac. ▪

☛ **WHAT · TO · SEE** From the Maryland side of the Potomac, where the battle was fought, when the leaves have fallen from the trees, you may be able to see the cascading waterfall from which the town across the river and the battle get their names. The area on the Maryland side where the road led down to the pontoon bridge used by Confederates is not readily apparent. From the village of Falling Waters in West Virginia, however, you can get a better view of the small waterfall and the private boat launching ramp just below it. Most of the riverbank on the West Virginia side of the Potomac consists of a bluff or cliff and would not have been used by the marching troops of the Confederate Army or their wagons and artillery. Often, modern boat launching facilities have appeared where older roads leading to rivers have been, and the best guess as to where the Confederates crossed to the town of Falling Waters is where the modern, private boat launching ramp descends into the river. Upon close examination from the West Virginia side of the Potomac, using the private boat ramp as a guide, a trace road descending into the river on the Maryland side is discernable opposite the ramp. It is most likely that this is the span of river across which Lee's pontoon bridge at Falling Waters was laid.

SHEPHERDSTOWN

One wet day . . . I was crossing from Shepherdstown, when I found him [one "Isaac Smith"] at the foot of the hill which rises from the river, with an overloaded two-horse wagon. He told me he was hauling miner's tools for prospecting and needed help. I went up home, got my father's carriage horses and their driver, Enoch, and with their aid Mr. Smith's wagon was taken a mile over the hills toward Sharpsburg, his best route home. Being very young, I was much impressed with the grateful simplicity of the venerable actor as we parted in the rain and mud, with many dignified expressions of thanks on his part. I had not a suspicion that he was other than he seemed. But it was not very long until I found out that the rickety wagon contained boxes of "John Brown's pikes" and that I was an innocent particeps criminis in their introduction into Maryland. He had brought them from a station on the Baltimore and Ohio Railroad in Virginia, to which they had been shipped from New England.[4]

Henry Kyd Douglas, author of those words, was to become the youngest member of Stonewall Jackson's staff. He had grown up at Ferry Hill plantation, the large, columned mansion across the Potomac from Shepherdstown. Unknowingly he had helped John Brown, the ardent, militant abolitionist, as Brown was secretly

SHEPHERDSTOWN CAN BE reached from Martinsburg, West Virginia, by following Route 45 east or from Boonsboro and Sharpsburg, Maryland, by following Route 34 southwest. From Shepherdstown, cross the Potomac to Maryland on Route 34 and make an immediate right on the C & O Canal access road. A dirt road called the Canal Road leaves the parking area and runs along the C & O Canal. Some walking accesses to the canal can be seen off this road. By following the C & O Canal downstream along Canal Road about a mile from the parking lot, almost exactly between mile markers 71 and 72, the remnants of the dam just upstream from Boteler's Ford can be located. Killiansburg Cave, along with several other overhangs referred to as "caves," are located upstream from Shepherdstown about 2.5 miles between mile 75.5 and 76.5 on the C & O Canal. Directly across from the canal access road is the driveway to Ferry Hill, now the home of the National Park Service administering the C & O Canal.

gathering weapons for the army of slaves he was expecting to lead in a war against their masters. But rather than leading his slave army to their own freedom, Brown instead became one of the sparks that set the great conflagration of the American Civil War, and young Henry Kyd Douglas inadvertently became caught up in it. Douglas would later participate in the making of history himself on the staff of one of the major participants and would record that history in his book, *I Rode with Stonewall.*

Shepherdstown played its most important part in the Civil War during the Battle of Antietam, but because of its location on the Potomac, it was occupied by contingents of both sides throughout the four years of war. It was the adopted home of Wesley Culp, from the small Pennsylvania farm town of Gettysburg, who had moved to Shepherdstown before the war with his employer, a carriage-maker. Culp, no doubt to make friends in his new home, joined the local militia outfit, the Hamtramck Guards. With them he spent many a carefree Sunday afternoon, drilling before the ladies of Shepherdstown, then eating barbecue in the Southern style in his pretty new militia uniform. When the war broke out, the Hamtramck Guards enlisted

---

☛ **W H A T · T O · S E E** The road and hill mentioned by Douglas lead from the spot where a covered bridge stood until burned by Confederates in 1861, about three-quarters of a mile from mile marker 72. This location is more easily accessed by taking the road leading down to the river off Route 34, across from Ferry Hill, now the National Park Service's Headquarters for administering the C & O Canal. The hill down to the river and canal is indeed formidable, and one huge, dead, twisted tree, which doubtless witnessed the events described by Douglas, still stands halfway up the hill.

Between miles 75.5 and 76.5 on the C & O Canal towpath are a series of caves, the largest of which is called Killiansburg Cave. Local legend has it that the townsfolk of Sharpsburg, two miles away, huddled in these caves to escape the carnage occurring just outside their town on September 17, 1862.

Much of Shepherdstown has been caught up in the preservation movement of the last several years, and many of the houses have been restored to their early appearance. The quaint town boasts several good restaurants and a large number of shops and stores. A few hours spent in Shepherdstown dining and walking are well worth the time.

in what they believed would be a short-lived Confederate Army. They became a part of a brigade of other Virginians commanded by a prosaic, dour former professor from Virginia Military Institute named Thomas J. Jackson. The *nom de guerre* he earned in his first battle would stick as well to his old brigade even after Jackson was gone: "The Stonewall Brigade." Marching on an invasion in the summer of 1863, Culp found himself in his old hometown of Gettysburg again, on his uncle's farm near a hill named after his own family. But Culp had come home to Gettysburg only to be killed and buried, never to see Shepherdstown again, and the rocky loam upon which he had played as a child became his burial ground. Culp's former captain and friend, Henry Kyd Douglas, would fall wounded on that same bloody hill. ▪

ANTIETAM

THE ANTIETAM NATIONAL BATTLE-field is located near Sharpsburg, Maryland, about a half-hour drive from Harpers Ferry. It is the scene of what has been called the bloodiest day in American history.[5]

Antietam Creek empties into the Potomac, and the fact that Lee had the Potomac River at his back gave him one more worry during the battle: Should rain raise the level of the river while he was facing the enemy, Lee would have little room to maneuver for battle and could be driven by his adversary, Union general George McClellan, into a dangerous pocket.

On September 17, 1862, Lee skillfully fought his army all day against a much larger Union army. As his right flank was about to be overrun, Con-

SHARPSBURG, MARYLAND, CAN be reached from the north by following Maryland Route 65 south from Hagerstown, Maryland, and from the west by following Route 45 east from Martinsburg to Shepherdstown, West Virginia. Cross the Potomac at Shepherdstown and follow Maryland Route 34 to Sharpsburg. From the east, follow U.S. Route 40 west from Frederick, then alternate U.S. 40 to Boonsboro, where you can take Route 34 southwest to Sharpsburg. From the south, take U.S. Route 340 east from Harpers Ferry, first crossing the Shenandoah River, then the Potomac. Once across

continued on page 20

federate general A. P. Hill—of the flaming red "battle-shirt"—arrived on the field after a seventeen-mile forced march from Harpers Ferry to bolster Lee's right. On their retreat, Lee and his army recrossed into Virginia (now West Virginia) over Boteler's Ford on the Potomac below Shepherdstown. ▪

continued from page 19
the Potomac, follow the signs to Sandy Hook and the Kennedy Farm, where John Brown lived before his raid. Take this country road (called Harpers Ferry Road) along the Potomac, following the signs to Sharpsburg or the Antietam Battlefield. Once you are in Sharpsburg, signs will direct you to the battlefield.

☛ **W H A T · T O · S E E**   Although a thorough study of the Battle of Antietam can take years, plan at least three hours to see the National Park Service Visitor Center and exhibits and to drive the park roads to the various main battle sites.

Boteler's Ford

BOTELER'S FORD

ACROSS BOTELER'S (ALSO KNOWN AS Packhorse, Shepherdstown, or Blackford's) Ford, the shallow, rocky part of the river, General Lee and his battered Army of Northern Virginia retreated after the bloody Battle of Antietam in September 1862. A low dam just upstream from the ford was used by Union soldiers of the 118th Pennsylvania, mauled by Lee's rear guard when the Pennsylvanians tried to fight with defective rifles, on their hasty retreat back across the river.

Thomas F. Hahn, in his towpath guidebook of the C & O Canal, states that the dam and accompanying mill-race once supplied waterpower to the lime cement mill located across the river from the towpath. The mill was burned by Union soldiers on August 19, 1861. The dam also provided deep water for boats carrying the finished cement across to the canal. From there it was transported upstream or down, some of it apparently ending up in many of the government buildings that were built in Washington, D.C.,

B Y WALKING ABOUT A MILE downstream on the towpath that begins at the parking area for the C & O Canal across the river from Shepherdstown, you can reach Boteler's Ford, where Stonewall Jackson's men crossed the Potomac on their way to the Battle of Antietam, and where Lee's bloodied army retreated after the battle. The remnants of the dam are between mile markers 71 and 72. Access can also be made by automobile by following Canal Road, the dirt road leading downstream from the C & O Canal parking area, just off Route 34. Drive one mile down Canal Road, park, and walk across the dry canal bed to the river. The dam and ford are slightly downstream from the cement kiln arches on the other side of the river.

possibly including the Washington Monument.[6] ▪

> ☞ **W H A T · T O · S E E** Boteler's Ford can be seen just downstream of the remains of the old dam, which can be distinguished by the straight line of ripples across the Potomac. At low water, the dam itself can be seen. The arched cement kilns are visible across the Potomac at the opposite side of the dam along with an anticline, a natural geologic arch, in the rock strata just downstream from the dam.

HARPERS FERRY

ON OCTOBER 17, 1859, LT. COL. Robert E. Lee was home at the Custis Mansion at Arlington Heights, Virginia, when a young U.S. Army lieutenant he had known while serving as superintendent at the U.S. Military Academy arrived to deliver a message from the War Department across the river. He told Lee that some insurgents had captured the U.S. Armory at Harpers Ferry, Virginia, and that Lee was to travel there and take command of the troops. The young lieutenant, sensing military action, volunteered as an aide to Lee. It wouldn't be the last time Jeb Stuart would serve under Lee.

Sheer cliffs and steep hillsides mark the meeting of the Shenandoah River and the Potomac. A tongue of land between the two was settled in the eighteenth century, then chosen as the site for a U.S. armory because of the power the rushing waters would provide. A geological cataclysm had caused the waters to converge there, and in October 1859 a man named John Brown chose Harpers Ferry for the man-made cataclysm that was to divide the United States.

Brown felt that he had been chosen as God's instrument to rid the nation of the sin of human bondage. He had dipped his hands in blood before, in Kansas during the terrorism over the

HARPERS FERRY IS REACHED BY following Route 340 from Maryland, West Virginia, or Virginia. A unique view of Harpers Ferry can be seen from the C & O Canal between mile markers 60 and 62. Access to that stretch of the C & O Canal as well as lock #33 is made either from Harpers Ferry by crossing the Potomac on the footbridge at "The Point," next to the railroad bridge, or from the Maryland side from the Harpers Ferry Road leading upstream on the Maryland side of the Potomac from Sandy Point (also marked as the road to the Kennedy Farm).

vote as to whether the state should be slave or free. He and his sons killed five proslavery men with axes. His plan this time was more grandiose: to capture the armory and its weapons, wait for the word of his mission to get out and the slaves to flock to him, then lead them as an army to their freedom.

His plans for a slave uprising beginning at Harpers Ferry fell apart almost before they began. The first man killed in the assault on Harpers Ferry was a freed black. Brown's band found themselves holed up in the fire engine house rather than the armory, pinned down by fire from angry townspeople. And the word to the slaves to join him didn't get out fast enough, or else many of the slaves were hesitant to join some wild scheme for a concept that, for most of them, was just a long-forgotten dream.

When Lee arrived at Harpers Ferry, he took charge of the U.S. Marines who had been transported there from the Navy Yard in Washington, still in their dress uniforms, not fully understanding that they would be going into action. After a brief parley with Brown demanding his surrender, Stuart signaled to Lee that Brown was not going to come out. Lee ordered the marines to assault the engine house. The battle lasted about three minutes. Brown was captured and two of his followers were killed. Brown was tried

and sentenced by November 2, 1859, and was hanged at Charles Town, Virginia, on December 2.

In September 1862, Gen. Stonewall Jackson, by order of General Lee, set artillery upon the heights around the town to induce the Union force encamped within Harpers Ferry to surrender. The Union troops there represented a large enemy force in the rear of Lee's advance as he moved through the area on his 1862 Maryland Campaign. Jackson advanced toward the town when a flag of truce was seen. Union general White came out and surrendered his entire garrison—11,000 Yankee officers and men, one of the largest wholesale captures of United States troops in American history. ▪

☛ **WHAT · TO · SEE** Harpers Ferry is an excellent place to begin a tour of some of the Civil War–related sites along the upper Potomac. The National Park Service at Harpers Ferry National Historical Site runs shuttle buses for walking tours into the restored historic town. Privately owned craft and gift shops are located on the streets leading up to Bolivar Heights behind and above the historic town. The view from the Hilltop House, from which you can see three states—Maryland, Virginia, and West Virginia—beneath you, is truly marvelous. From Harpers Ferry, most of the sites on the upper Potomac are within an hour's drive.

WHITE'S FORD

ROBERT E. LEE AND HIS INVADING army crossed at White's Ford during his Antietam Campaign, September 6, 1862.[7] Eleven days later the army would be fighting for its life near Sharpsburg, Maryland, and Antietam Creek in a battle named for the town by Southerners and after the creek by Northerners.

At White's Ford near the mouth of the Monocacy was also where Confederate cavalry commander Jeb Stuart recrossed the Potomac on October 12, 1862, after his three-day raid into Pennsylvania. The area just east of the ford was the site of much consternation for Jeb Stuart, as well as a clever ruse played by the Confederates, before they could cross the rapidly rising Potomac.

By the morning of October 12, 1862, Stuart's troopers were exhausted but jubilant after having conducted one of the more daring cavalry raids in the Civil War. They had left Darksville, Virginia (now West Virginia), on October 9 and crossed the Potomac at 4 A.M. on October 10 at McCoy's Ferry (mile marker 110.5). They pounded across the Pennsylvania line and by dark had captured Chambersburg, Pennsylvania. Along the way they gathered horses, food, and clothing, much of it Union blue, which

WHITE'S FORD IS LOCATED between C & O Canal mile markers 39.5 and 39.6. Closest access is from canal lock #26. The easiest way to find this lock is to get on the canal towpath at Dickerson Regional Park and hike downstream.

By automobile, White's Ford can be reached by following Route 28 south out of Dickerson, Maryland. At the flashing light bear right on the Martinsburg Road, and follow it about 1.2 miles to the fork with Wausch Road. Bear right and remain on Martinsburg Road for about 2 miles. Turn right at the sign for "Dickerson Conservation Park," and follow this back road about .4 miles to a parking lot at the end.

they gladly donned to replace their tattered gray and butternut uniforms. In Chambersburg they burned the government depot, machine shops, firearms, and a warehouse of ammunition, which exploded through the morning.[8] But they failed in their efforts to burn the Cumberland Valley Railroad bridge spanning the Conococheague, a main line of communications from southern Pennsylvania to Harrisburg, the state capital. Though destroying the bridge was one of the specific objectives Robert E. Lee had mentioned in his orders to Stuart, it was constructed of iron and resistant to the torch.

Swinging in a wide arc to the west and south, Stuart and his troopers passed near Gettysburg then approached the Potomac in Maryland on a little-known farm road, exhausted from an all-night march and hoping to cross at White's Ford with their booty.

Less than a mile from the river they bumped headlong into a column of Union cavalry. A lesser officer might have tried to determine the strength of the enemy by sending out vedettes, then attempted to work his way around their flanks by dismounting his men. But Stuart himself was commanding the Confederate column. He and his advanced troopers charged and drove the Yankees from their front; then they climbed the ridge overlooking the Little Monocacy River and saw Union troopers digging in.

Stuart sent Gen. William H. F. "Rooney" Lee—son of Robert E. Lee—with the main column toward White's Ford; Stuart himself, along with the famous Confederate artillerist John Pelham, would handle the most dangerous part of the crossing, the rearguard action.

Near the ford was a quarry, its rim lined with Union riflemen ready to fire on a column exposed in the open water at the ford. Rooney Lee's original plan was to attack the quarry and keep the enemy occupied while a small group of horsemen and some artillery forced a crossing at the ford and set up positions on the other side to cover it. Moments mattered because the recent rains were swelling the Potomac and covering the ford with deeper and deeper water. Yet men's lives mattered too. Lee sent a note under a flag of truce to the Union commander stating that Gen. Jeb Stuart himself was present with a huge cavalry force, and if surrender wasn't made in a quarter hour, the Confederates would attack.

The fifteen minutes passed. Lee

☞ **W H A T · T O · S E E** The vicinity of White's Ford is protected as a regional park. Several quarries are in the area and along the Martinsburg Road down to Dickerson Regional Park, any one of which could be the one used by Union soldiers against Rooney Lee's troopers. The path across the C & O Canal from the parking area down to the river gives a good view of the large bend in the Potomac, the shallowest and narrowest portion of which was used by Confederates several times during the war.

began his advance after two Confederate cannons opened fire on the quarry. To the Confederates' surprise, the bluff worked and the Union troops began a withdrawal downstream. The ford was in Southern hands. Stuart had trouble drawing off his rear guard and at one point thought the men and cannons were lost to the enemy, but by 10 A.M. the Confederates were safely across the river and into Virginia. ▪

WHITE'S FERRY

WHITE'S FERRY IS THE LAST REMAINING ferry of nearly one hundred regularly operating ferry boats that once plied the Potomac at various crossings. It was originally called Conrad's Ferry, but the name was changed when Lt. Col. E. V. White, a Virginian, took over the ferry business after the Civil War.[9] White commanded the 35th Virginia Cavalry Battalion in Gen. "Grumble" Jones's Brigade during the Gettysburg Campaign in the summer of 1863.[10] ▪

WHITE'S FERRY IS AT ABOUT the 35.5 mile marker on the C & O Canal. It can be reached from the Maryland side of the Potomac by taking White's Ferry Road west from Poolesville. On the Virginia side of the river, White's Ferry can be reached from U.S. Route 15 just north of the Leesburg bypass by taking county road 655 east about 1.3 miles until it dead-ends at the ferry.

☞ **WHAT · TO · SEE** The ferry is still used as the quickest means to commute across the river by a large number of Marylanders who work in Washington and Virginia. On pleasant weekends, bicyclists from Virginia use the facility as a quaint, convenient way to reach the C & O Canal for recreational purposes.

1,000 men in the debacle, but the Confederates lost only about 150. General Stone was given the blame and Baker became a martyr, and rumors of blue-clad, bloated bodies floating lazily down the Potomac to Washington were rife. ▪

HARRISON'S ISLAND

IN ADDITION TO BEING THE LOCATION of an early settlement and fort in the first few years of the eighteenth century, Harrison's Island was also the temporary campsite for some Tuscarora Native Americans for two seasons beginning in 1711.

But the Civil War came to Harrison's Island in October 1861. It was from this island in the Potomac that Col. Edward Baker sent his troops across in his ill-conceived assault on Ball's Bluff on the Virginia side of the river. It was to Harrison's Island that a number of them—the lucky ones, at least—swam to escape the Confederates' fire from above. Local legends

HARRISON'S ISLAND LIES IN THE Potomac between C & O Canal mile markers 33 and 35 on the Maryland side on the river. It can also be seen from the bottom of the path leading from the Ball's Bluff National Cemetery parking lot on the Virginia side of the Potomac.

reaching back to the canal days say that this area is haunted by the disgruntled spirits of those who were drowned in the river during the retreat. Canal boatmen avoided tying up overnight in this area if possible. ▪

☞ **W H A T · T O · S E E** Harrison's Island is the far shore (only about 100 yards) from where the walking path from the Ball's Bluff National Cemetery ends at the Potomac. It is one of the largest islands in the Potomac—almost two miles long—and therefore appears to be the opposite shoreline. From the Virginia shore, nothing can be seen on the island except a silo, a barn, and some farm fields. The fields are flat, and it is easy to imagine the Massachusetts and New York troops lining up to take their small boats across the Potomac and then floundering in the water as they attempted to swim back to Harrison's Island.

EDWARD'S FERRY

THOUGH THE FERRYBOAT THAT crossed the Potomac at this point had ceased operation by 1836, the area continued to be called Edward's Ferry, and it remained one of the more important crossings of the Potomac. Of importance to early commerce using Edward's Ferry was a small pivot bridge that spanned the C & O Canal. Without this bridge, a traveler would have had to make a six-mile detour to White's Ferry to cross the canal.[11]

The Civil War almost wore out the old canal bridge with heavy loads of infantry, cavalry, and artillery. Some of the Federal Army of the Potomac crossed at Edward's Ferry on pontoon

EDWARD'S FERRY IS ABOUT two-tenths of a mile downstream from mile marker 31 and at lock #25, accessible from Poolesville, Maryland, by going west on White's Ferry Road (Maryland Route 107) about two miles and turning left on Edward's Ferry Road.

bridges during the Gettysburg Campaign in pursuit of Lee's invading Army of Northern Virginia.[12] Confederate general Jubal Early's cavalry crossed here on its way back from Early's raid to the gates of Washington in July 1864. ∎

Edward's Ferry was the scene of numerous crossings during the war.

☛ **W H A T · T O · S E E** Remnants of lock #25 on the C & O Canal are still visible at Edward's Ferry, and remains of a bypass flume and boat basin just above the lock await those who wish to explore the area in detail. Also standing is the restored lock house and the brick shell of Jarboe's store, which once supplied local farmers and canal boats with goods. There is a ramp for boaters and fishermen who want access to the Potomac. Check with local authorities concerning boating on this stretch of the Potomac; the river appears to be of variable depth with some dams and fords restricting boat traffic.

Notes

1. Hahn, 5–9.
2. Thomason, 300–19.
3. Coddington, 565–72.
4. Douglas, 14.
5. Frassanito, *Antietam*, 17.
6. Hahn, 122–23.
7. Murfin, 90.
8. Davis, 216–34.
9. Hahn, 72.
10. Coddington, 166.
11. Hahn, 65.
12. Nesbitt, 121.

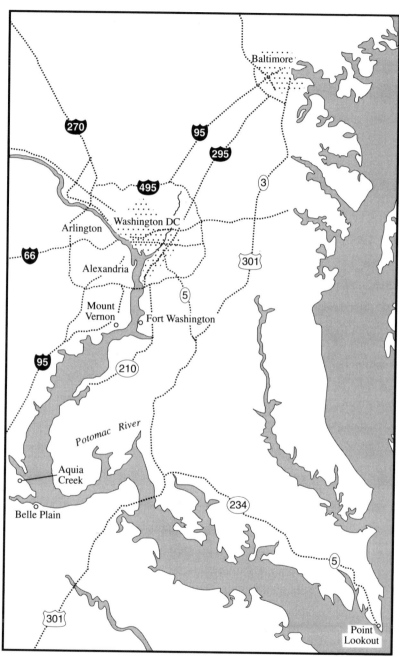

The Lower Potomac River

✦ THE LOWER ✦ POTOMAC RIVER

THE LOWER POTOMAC was important not only as a barrier to hostile armies, as was the upper Potomac, but also as a potential means of rapid deployment of artillery, troops, and matériel for both armies. Huge guns mounted upon ships could back up and protect either army operating close to the navigable lower portion of the Potomac. Until the summer of 1862, Confederates manned forts and positions on the Virginia side of the lower Potomac, but the river is so wide there that their artillery couldn't close the river off completely from the Union Navy.

Union troops and supplies could be loaded at Alexandria's extensive wharves, after Alexandria had been captured by Federal forces, and shipped from there to virtually anywhere along the nation's coast. Like the James, the Potomac would become a massive highway for whichever navy controlled it.

ARLINGTON

YOUNG MARY ANNE RANDOLPH Custis, descendant of George Washington's family, had married twenty-four-year-old Robert E. Lee at the Custis family mansion at Arlington on June 30, 1831, and it was in her home on the hill at Arlington they chose to live. On outpost duty for much of his early years in the army,

ARLINGTON IS REACHED FROM Washington, D.C., via the Memorial Bridge, from the south via Route 95, from the north by taking the Washington Beltway (I-495) to the George Washington Memorial Parkway, or from the west via Route 50 or 66.

33

Lee tried to understand why his wife spent much of her time at her childhood home rather than with him. But the rough barracks provided to the army wives told the story. She had led a pampered life and loved Arlington. Lee also learned to love the great, columned mansion on the hill at Arlington and considered it his home as well.

On May 23, 1861, Virginians ratified the ordinance of secession from the Union. That night, 13,000 Union troops crossed the Potomac on the Long Bridge to capture Arlington Heights overlooking the Capital. They found the lovely mansion on the hill deserted. Lee had lately resigned from the U.S. Army to cast his lot with his native state of Virginia and was away on duty. Warned by a relative on the staff of the Union general-in-chief and encouraged by Lee, the Lee women had packed all their

---

☛ **W H A T · T O · S E E** The extensive National Cemetery at Arlington holds the remains of thousands of American heroes, including numerous Congressional Medal of Honor recipients, general officers, the Unknown Soldiers, and 250 Confederate soldiers. Tourmobiles shuttle visitors around the huge cemetery.

Arlington House has been restored and is administered by the National Park Service. It contains memorabilia of the Lee family, including the original portrait of Mary Anne Randolph Custis before she became Mrs. Robert E. Lee. It hangs in the room where the couple was married. Copies of original portraits of various family members hang in the other rooms. The upstairs bedchambers and Lee's office are open to the public, as is the north wing of the mansion, which contains a kitchen, a children's schoolroom, and the Custis's bedchambers. Outside Arlington House are the servants' quarters, gardens, and a small museum depicting the life of Robert E. Lee.

While visiting the mansion and grounds, don't pass up the opportunity to enjoy the magnificent view of Washington from the front porch. Beneath your feet are the original pavers trod upon by the Custis and Lee family members and guests as well as countless numbers of Union soldiers once they took over the grounds. The Memorial Bridge below was located specifically to connect visually the Lincoln Memorial with Arlington House as a symbol of a nation united.

valuables—including some of the priceless heirlooms from the George Washington family—and abandoned Arlington. Union officers and men pitched tents in the yard and cut down the magnificent trees, though they avoided the mansion on specific orders from their commander.

Yet the respect given to the Custis's mansion because of its association with a descendant of Washington did not last long. Because of Robert E. Lee's growing prominence as commander of the Army of Northern Virginia, Arlington House (Lee's name for the mansion) was finally confiscated by the U.S. government in January 1864. Oddly, Arlington House and the surrounding grounds were purchased by the government for three-quarters of the assessed value because the owners did not pay their taxes in person, as required by a recently enacted law. Obviously, with the war going on, General Lee could not appear in Washington to pay, nor could Mrs. Lee, an invalid. A cousin attempted to pay the taxes on Arlington House but was sent away by the U.S. government. Within six months, Federal soldiers were being buried, by order of Gen. Montgomery Meigs, as close to the mansion as possible so as to make its reoccupation by the Lees—if that should ever happen—as odious as possible.[1] ▪

ALEXANDRIA

On May 24, 1861, the day after Virginia seceded, Union forces were ordered into Alexandria, Virginia. Alexandria would become the embarkation point for thousands of Union troops bound for the battlefields in Virginia. Many of the same happy troops leaving for the great adventure of war would return to the Alexandria wharves torn and limbless, immeasurably scarred by their experience. ▪

Alexandria can be reached by following Route 50 or 29 from the west to Route 236 (the Little River Turnpike), from the south by following Route 95 or 1 (to Old Town Alexandria), from the north by following Route 495 to 95 to Route 1, or from the east by getting on Route 95 toward Virginia and exiting onto Route 1.

☞ **W H A T · T O · S E E** Old Town Alexandria, restored and looking very much like it did to young Robert E. Lee when he grew up there, is a delightful place to spend a Saturday afternoon. Alexandria was originally a trading center for tobacco and shipbuilding. Among the Civil War sites to see are Robert E. Lee's boyhood home and the site of the Marshall House, scene of one of the first casualties in the American Civil War. Numerous other places to visit abound in Alexandria, and a number of cruises on the Potomac are available and are recommended as the way to see the city as the Union soldiers did when they left for the Peninsula Campaign.

A brochure entitled *Walking Tour Guide of Old Town* is available from the Alexandria Convention & Visitors Bureau, 221 King Street, Alexandria, VA 22314. The tour includes many of the sites associated with the Civil War and the Potomac River.

MOUNT VERNON

As their vessels passed Mount Vernon, Union soldiers aboard ships transporting them to and from Alexandria would pause and salute in homage to the country's first president, George Washington. The tradition continues to this day.

In 1669 George Washington's great-grandfather John Washington obtained a patent for some five thousand acres along the Potomac shore. Approximately one-half of the property devolved through inheritance through the family, until it was sold in 1726 to Augustine Washington by his sister, Mildred. Augustine built a house on the estate in 1735 and

Mount Vernon can be reached by following Virginia Route 235 off of U.S. Route 1, or by taking the Mount Vernon Memorial Highway south out of Alexandria. Cyclists or hikers may want to try the Mount Vernon Trail, a paved pathway that runs 17 miles from the Lincoln Memorial to Mount Vernon. Boaters can see Mount Vernon as hundreds of thousands of Union soldiers saw it off of buoy G "71" Fl G. (Note: Not for navigational purposes. Caution: The water toward Mount

continued on page 37

moved there with his three-year-old son, George, but moved again just three years later to Ferry Farm. George's half-brother, Lawrence, inherited the property in 1743 and constructed a house for his new wife, no doubt on the foundation of Augustine's old house, which had burned. Lawrence called the new house Mount Vernon after his old commander in the British Navy.

George came to the spacious plantation along the Potomac when he was sixteen to live with his brother and wife. When Lawrence died he left the place to his daughter, Sarah, and when she died, George inherited the property, eventually buying up some adjacent lands.

In 1759 George Washington moved to Mount Vernon with his bride, Martha, wishing to develop his skills in farming. He divided the land into

continued from page 36
Vernon is very shallow and has a narrow dredged channel marked by buoys. Consult NOS charts and publications, Local Notices to Mariners, and local boaters before attempting to cruise this area.)

five separate farms, experimenting with new techniques, rotating crops, and keeping details of his progress. A third story was added to the house in 1773, and plans were drawn for north and south wings. But as the rebellion broke out, Washington was called from his home to command the army of the colonies on the continent.

After the war he returned to farming, but after just four years he was called to his country's service once again to preside at the Constitutional Convention in 1787. The presidency

☛ **W H A T · T O · S E E** A magnificent view of the Potomac can be enjoyed from the columned portico of Mount Vernon. Washington's home holds numerous original furnishings and artifacts of the first president. Mount Vernon boasts a library, archives, a map collection, genealogical records of the Washington and Custis families, and a curatorial collection. The tomb of George and Martha Washington can be seen during the tour of the grounds. The museum is open at 9:00 A.M. daily and closes at 4:00 P.M. November through February and at 5:00 P.M. March through October. Admission is $7.00 for adults, $3.00 for children ages 6–11, and $6.00 for senior citizens.

of the new nation drew him away from his beloved farming until 1797. After he returned to Mount Vernon, he had but two years in which to enjoy the bucolic life along the shore of the great river. Washington died on December 14, 1799, and was buried at Mount Vernon.[2]

According to the Mount Vernon Ladies Association, organized before the Civil War to preserve the house and grounds where Washington lived, both Union and Confederate soldiers often visited the mansion, their uniforms sometimes disguised under shawls. There is a tree on the premises that bears the carvings of at least one Civil War soldier. ▪

AQUIA CREEK

AQUIA CREEK LANDING, IN THE FIRST months of 1863, was the major supply base for Gen. Ambrose Burnside's Union army as it was encamped in Falmouth, Virginia, across the Rappahannock from Fredericksburg. The Fredericksburg and Potomac Railroad had its northern terminus at Aquia Creek Station, which appears on modern nautical charts as Thorney Point (and "Thorny Point" on the atlas to the *Official Records*). By the time U. S. Grant began his Virginia Campaign in the spring of 1864, the railroad between Aquia Creek and Fredericksburg had been destroyed, and Grant had shifted his base of supplies from Aquia to Belle Plain, a few miles downstream on Potomac Creek. ▪

AQUIA CREEK CAN BE REACHED off U.S. Route 1, north of Fredericksburg, Virginia, by a number of local county roads. At Stafford, Virginia, turn east on Route 630. Take Route 629 southward to 608, and 608 to Thorney Point on Route 685. Boaters can enter Aquia Creek from the Potomac by rounding buoy "2" Fl R 4sec 15ft, keeping to the south of it to avoid shallow water to the north. Follow the markers to buoy "12" Fl R 2 1/2sec 15ft. (Note: Not for navigational purposes. Buoys may change position and numbering systems may be altered. Consult current NOS charts and publications, Local Notices to Mariners, and local boaters before cruising these waters.)

☞ **W H A T · T O · S E E** The "Landing" at Aquia Creek is shown approximately 1.75 miles upstream from Thorney Point. The railroad now runs more to the north and crosses Aquia Creek about 2.5 miles upstream from the Point. No mapped roads run to the area shown as the landing, but boaters can see the area to port once they pass the buoy marked "12" Fl R 2 1/2 sec 15ft off Thorney Point.

BELLE PLAIN

By springtime 1864, Grant's engineers had corduroyed roads in the area of Belle Plain while they were attempting to rebuild the Aquia Creek/ Fredericksburg railway. In mid-May Belle Plain became a funnel through which supplies and personnel from Washington and Alexandria flowed. But because Grant moved so swiftly, fighting battles at the Wilderness and Spotsylvania and leapfrogging the right flank of Lee's army, by May 28 his base of supplies had already been shifted three times: first from Aquia Creek to Belle Plain on Potomac Creek; then to Port Royal on the Rappahannock; then, on May 28, to White House on the Pamunkey, a tributary of the York River. By June 9, 1864, Grant would be in the process of shifting his base again, to City Point on the James.

But from May 10 until May 20, when the Rappahannock was opened to Union gunboats and Port Royal

To reach Belle Plain, take Route 218 east out of Fredericksburg, Virginia, turn left on county Route 600, then follow the signs to Waugh Point. By boat, enter Potomac Creek, staying close to buoy "2" Fl R 4sec 15ft, and follow the daymarks into the creek. Daymark G "5" is just off the first point where the pontoon wharf was located, and daymark G "7" appears to be just off where the second pontoon wharf was placed. (Note: Not for navigational purposes. Always consult current NOS charts and publications, Local Notices to Mariners, and local boaters before attempting a cruise.)

could be used as a base, Belle Plain (along with Fredericksburg) not only became the ferrying point to Washington for some 26,000 wounded Union

Belle Plain

☛ **WHAT·TO·SEE** Belle Plain is now called Waugh Point by locals and appears as such on certain modern nautical charts. It, and the roads leading to it, fail to appear on modern state road maps of Virginia. Waugh Point is well back a one-lane dirt road that ends at a private marina. The marina has no overnight or transient slips for boaters, this area of Potomac Creek being off the beaten path of most weekend cruisers. The gentleman who owns the marina was friendly and knowledgeable and pointed out that he was under the impression that one pontoon wharf, where tons of supplies arrived for the army, extended from the spot where his modern dock is anchored, and another pontoon wharf extended from a point several hundred yards west. He also acknowledged that numerous people (probably relic hunters) have quizzed him about the location of the Punch Bowl, but no one has discovered its location. I visited there in November when all the leaves were gone from the trees and felt I recognized the Punch Bowl from old photographs—at least two or three times! The ground from Route 218 to Potomac Creek is cut by draws and undulating "bowls" of hillocks and valleys, so what appears to be the historic area jumps out every two or three miles. Even historian William Frassanito, who has conducted exhaustive research, thought the area impossible to find, although he may have come the closest to locating it. His detailed photographic analysis places it fairly close to the creek.[5]

troops, but was also a holding pen for several thousand Confederate soldiers captured in the fighting at the Wilderness and Spotsylvania.[3] Many of the Confederate enlisted men were on their way to Point Lookout and the prison camp there. Officers would be taken to Fort Delaware.

While at Belle Plain, Confederate prisoners were kept in a series of undulating gorges just back from the river, where they could all be accounted for at a glance by their Union guards. This huge depression was called the "Punch Bowl" and was documented photographically by James Gardner and Mathew Brady's assistants.[4] ∎

FORT WASHINGTON

FORT WASHINGTON STANDS ON THE site of old Fort Warburton, which was constructed in 1809. The location for the fort was chosen in 1794 by George Washington, who was no doubt familiar with this section of the Potomac since his home, Mount Vernon, is located just one and one-half miles downstream on the Virginia side of the river.

Fort Warburton (by then also known as Fort Washington) was destroyed by the American commander in August 1814 before it could fall into British hands during their attack upon Washington during the War of 1812.

Just twelve days after the destruction of the old fort, construction of the present Fort Washington was begun. The designer of the city of Washington, a French engineer, Maj. Pierre L'Enfant, began clearing away debris from the destroyed old fort and started

TO REACH FORT WASHINGTON from the north, west, or east, follow Route 495 to Maryland Route 210 south of Washington, then follow 210 south to Fort Washington Road. From the south, cross the Potomac into Maryland and follow 210 north. Fort Washington can be seen by boaters from the Potomac at Piscataway Creek. The huge stone walls are unmistakable when nearing buoy "80" Fl R 6sec 28ft. (Note: Not for navigational purposes. Consult current NOS charts, Local Notices to Mariners, and local boaters before cruising this area.)

plans for the present Fort Washington.

Economic considerations led to L'Enfant's removal as chief engineer. He was replaced by Lt. Col. Walker K. Armistead, whose son Lewis would

☞ **W H A T · T O · S E E** Fort Washington remains a marvelous example of a massive fixed fortification, a type of military edifice that dominated warfare from the Middle Ages until its obsolescence during this century. The view of the Potomac River from the parapets of Fort Washington is indicative of the fort's importance as one of the main defenses for the Capital of the United States.

The National Park Service maintains exhibits, a bookstore, and some restored structures within the fort, and it provides a self-guided walking tour. Special seasonal tours are also available. The park is open daily from 7:30 A.M. until dark. The fort is open daily except December 25. From September 1 through April 30 the fort is open from 7:30 A.M. to 5 P.M.; from May 1 through August 31, hours are 7:30 A.M. to 8 P.M. The museum is open daily from June 1 to Labor Day and on holidays and weekends throughout the year.

Fort Washington

The Potomac River can be seen from the parapet of Fort Washington.

also become a soldier and would one day lead his Confederate soldiers across a low stone wall at the climax of Pickett's Charge at Gettysburg. By 1824 the fort was nearly complete. It appears today very much like it did then.

In January 1861, three months before hostilities broke out in the Civil War, a small contingent of U.S. Marines was sent to defend, if need be, the only fortification protecting the city of Washington at that time. Eventually, the Capital would be ringed with earthen forts and artillery. The construction in 1864, just below Alexandria on the Maryland shore of the river, of Fort Foote—built to withstand the new rifled artillery then in use—made Fort Washington obsolete. ∎

POINT LOOKOUT

IF THERE EVER WAS HELL ON THIS PIECE of earth called America, it was during the fury of a battle in the Civil War. And if there ever was anything worse than hell created here, it was a Civil War prison camp.

While the names Andersonville in Georgia, Libby in Richmond, and

FOLLOW MARYLAND ROUTE 5 from the Washington Beltway (I-495) or Maryland Route 3 from Baltimore until it becomes U.S. 301 and follow that south to Route 5. Take Maryland Route 5 southeast to Point Lookout.

Johnson's Island in Ohio are well known, less well known is the prison camp at Point Lookout, Maryland.

Point Lookout was first seen by Europeans in 1634 and named St. Michaels. A priest traveling along with the exploratory vessels *Ark* and *Dove* was impressed by the size of the Potomac River, calling the Thames a "rivulet" compared to it. The settlers saw armed natives and fires that night all along the banks. Native American runners were sent out, calling others to come and see the "canoe" the size of an island anchored near the point.

Two hundred twenty-five years later, Point Lookout had become a summer resort, with a hundred or so cottages along the beach, catering to those mid-nineteenth-century Virginians and Marylanders who could afford the time off to vacation at the shore. A wharf and prominent lighthouse added to the pre–Civil War scene.

By August 1862, the U.S. government rented the Point Lookout resort as a hospital for wounded soldiers. By early 1863, Confederate prisoners were being sent to the point, and after the Battle of Gettysburg the construction of a prisoner-of-war camp with a capacity of 10,000 was begun. Typical of most prisoner-of-war camps in both North and South, the camp was soon crowded well over its capacity. By September 1863 there were 4,000

☛ **W H A T · T O · S E E** Other historic sites are located on this rural peninsula: St. Clements Island, site of the first landing of Maryland settlers in 1634; Port Tobacco, a restored nineteenth-century village; St. Mary's City, Maryland's first capital, with a restored seventeenth-century village and a replica of the *Dove*, one of the ships that carried the first settlers from England; and Lexington Park, home of the Patuxent River Naval Air Station and the Naval Air Test and Evaluation Museum.

Sometimes taking your time and following the backroads can lead to serendipitous discoveries. For example, John Wilkes Booth traveled through this section of Maryland on his flight south after assassinating President Abraham Lincoln. Booth traveled south after crossing the Potomac/Anacostia River over the Navy Yard Bridge (now the Anacostia River Bridge) to Surrattsville (now Clinton, Maryland); through the oddly named town of T.B.; to the vicinity of Waldorf, where he had his broken leg set by Doctor Samuel Mudd; and then to Pope's Creek, where he was rowed across the Potomac into Virginia.

prisoners interned at what was officially named Camp Hoffman; by December there were 9,000 prisoners; by June 1864 there were more than 20,000 men jammed into the camp; and by that winter some were literally freezing to death.

Of the total of 52,264 prisoners interned and released at one time or another at Point Lookout, 3,384 died and remain there to this day, buried under a large obelisk in the Confederate Cemetery.[6] ▪

CRUISING THE POTOMAC

SOME OF THE vistas from the water of the wooded shoreline still look much as they must have when Capt. John Smith explored the Potomac in the early seventeenth century, or when Union soldiers passed this way on their waterborne journey to Fort Monroe on the James River in Virginia before the Peninsula Campaign of 1862, or when other Union soldiers—replacements for those dead or wounded after three years of war—sailed down the Potomac to bolster Grant's army in 1864 and 1865.

This area of Maryland, with its numerous bays and large rivers emptying into the Potomac, is ideal for exploring by boat. The Potomac is five to six miles wide once it passes under the Route 301 bridge. Numerous marinas, campgrounds, and restaurants have been established all along the Maryland and Virginia shores of the Potomac, and overnight slips for boats usually run from $.90 to $1.50 a linear waterline foot with an extra charge for electrical hookup. Several have launch ramps if you wish to trailer to the marina for a day on the Potomac.

The Port Tobacco River is navigable up to the marina at its headwaters. St. Clements Island can be explored by tying up or beaching your vessel, and the new St. Clements Island Visitors Center, on the Maryland Shore across from the island, has a dock where you can tie up temporarily to see the exhibits housed there.

St. Mary's City has a lovely large bay below it with docks. Most of the exhibits at St. Mary's City are within walking distance from the bay.

At Point Lookout, there are no public ramp or docking facilities, but canoes and rowboats can be rented and launched at the Point Lookout State Park. A cruise boat can be taken to Smith Island for a fee.

On Occoquan Creek inside Occoquan Bay, there is a fine facility for launching or seasonal storage of your boat, several marinas, restaurants, and shopping areas. The state of Virginia has recently completed a large, four-bay ramp, parking facilities, and a seasonal fenced and lighted storage area for boats. A fee is charged for launching unless you are storing your boat for the season.

You will have a twenty-minute, no-wake cruise through Belmont Bay until the Potomac opens before you. A cruise upriver will take you past Mount Vernon, Fort Washington, Alexandria, Washington National Airport, and either up the Anacostia River or under the several bridges to Georgetown, passing the Kennedy Center and the Watergate Hotel on the way. This trip takes about two hours, one way, in a powerboat and is well marked by river channel buoys. Surprisingly, Washington, D.C., seemingly a sprawling, labyrinthine maze that takes forever to traverse by automobile, fits neatly in a big bend in the river when you view it from the Potomac.

Just across the river from Washington National Airport is Giesboro Point, where thousands of army horses for the artillery and remounts for the cavalry were bred.

Cruising downriver from Occoquan, you pass Quantico Marine Base, Aquia Creek, and Potomac Creek where Belle Plain is located, and at the bottom of the huge **S** formed by the river, Mathias Point is to starboard and Port Tobacco River to port. It was in this huge bend in the river that John Wilkes Booth's guide got lost. Instead of rowing the assassin straight across the Potomac from Pope's Creek (just downriver from Port Tobacco River) to Mathias Point in Virginia, Booth's boatman ended up rowing upriver and back into Maryland in Nanjemoy Creek. He did eventually get Booth to the Virginia shore, however.

If you want to cruise below the Route 301 bridge, you may want to plan for an overnighter, since there are several places of historical interest beyond, including St. Clements Island, St. Mary's City on the St. Mary's River, and Point Lookout.

A word of caution: The Potomac in this area is a large body of water and subject to all the hazards of any large, shallow river. Make sure your boat has adequate power—either motor or sail—as well as a compass and up-to-date charts. Phone ahead to marinas to reserve berth space prior to your arrival. The recommendations for cruising herein are merely suggested destination points and are not meant for navigational purposes. Consult up-to-date National Ocean Service charts and publications, and Local Notices to Mariners before taking any cruise on the Potomac River.

A Visitor's Guide to St. Mary's County is available by calling (301) 884-5555. The Guide to Charles County just northwest of St. Mary's County is available by calling the Chamber of Commerce at (301) 932-6500. Chesapeake Bay Communications sells an annual 350-page publication, *Guide to Cruising Chesapeake Bay*. It has a comprehensive listing, along with addresses and phone numbers, of marinas, restaurants, state parks, and facilities along both shores of the Potomac. Telephone (301) 263-2662 or write to Chesapeake Bay Communications, 1819 Bay Ridge Ave., Annapolis, MD 21403.

Notes

1. Coulling, 134.
2. *Virginia: A Guide to the Old Dominion*, 338–42.
3. Trudeau, 218.
4. Frassanito, *Grant and Lee*, 54.
5. *Ibid.*, 56.
6. Kemmerle, 1.

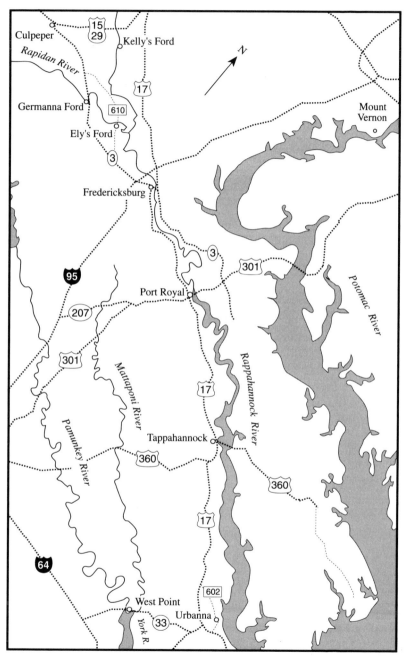

The Rappahannock River

✦ THE RAPPAHANNOCK ✦ RIVER

The country over which the army had to operate, from the Rapidan to the crossing of the James River, is rather flat, and is cut by numerous streams which make their way to the Chesapeake Bay. The crossings of these streams by the army were generally made not far above tide-water, and where they formed a considerable obstacle to the rapid advance of troops even when the enemy did not appear in opposition. The country roads were narrow and poor. Most of the country is covered with a dense forest, in places, like the Wilderness and along the Chickahominy, almost impenetrable even for infantry except along the roads. All bridges were naturally destroyed before the National troops came to them.[1]

THUS DID U. S. GRANT in his memoirs describe the land that drained into the Rappahannock, the York, and the James rivers, over which the Union Army had to march and fight to get to Lee's Army of Northern Virginia in 1864. The area had proved to be formidable, foreboding, and disastrous to several Union generals before Grant. He would move through the area so rapidly, however, that the flooding of streams and swamps by occasional rains, the destruction and necessary rebuilding of bridges, and brief, savage fighting in inhospitable woods would matter little to him.

Like the Potomac, the Rappahannock can be divided into two sections, upper and lower. The upper Rappahannock, its main tributary, the Rapidan, and the fords, bridges, and crossings along the length of these two until the river reaches Fredericksburg affected the two adversarial armies' tactics during 1862, 1863, and 1864 on a nearly hourly basis. Rappahannock Station, Kelly's Ford, Germanna Ford, Ely's Ford, United States Ford—these names are repeated time and again in official reports of the battles of Fredericksburg and Chancellorsville, the Gettysburg Campaign, and Grant's Virginia Campaign of 1864. And the navigable section of the Rappahannock below Fredericksburg sustains small port towns like Port Royal and Urbanna, names once known intimately by Lincoln and his cabinet, McClellan and Grant and their staffs, countless army telegraphers, and newspapermen from both sections of the country.

KELLY'S FORD ON THE UPPER RAPPAHANNOCK

UPSTREAM, WHERE THE RAPPAHANnock is only a hundred or so yards wide, is Kelly's Ford. Crossed and recrossed, and fought over several times, it was bitterly linked with the death in battle of one of the young heroes of the Confederacy, John Pelham. The Alabaman was in command of Jeb Stuart's Horse Artillery, and the shy, handsome young man had proved himself before the Confederate Army of Northern Virginia enough times to draw the attention of the commanding general himself. Lee at Fredericksburg wondered about a lone gun that kept firing despite being outnumbered and suffering incredible losses. Told it belonged to Pelham, he remarked, "It is glorious to see such courage in one so young!"[2] He would afterward

KELLY'S FORD CAN BE REACHED off business Route 15/29. Turn onto Route 673 just west of the Rappahannock River crossing at Rappahannock Station. Go about 2.3 miles and turn left at the crossroads onto 674. About 3.3 miles will take you to the Kelly's Ford area, and signs and a pathway lead you back to the ford.

refer to the youngster as "The Gallant Pelham."

On March 16, 1863, Pelham had met Stuart at Culpeper, Virginia, as the general testified in a court martial hearing. But young Pelham also visited the ladies, in particular Miss Bessie Shackleford, whose house stood on the northeast corner of Cameron and Main Streets in Culpeper.[3] It was a visit that would be cut short by impudent Yankee cavalry.

At dawn on March 17, 1863—a Sunday, the day in old Virginia for courting—Union general Averill's cavalry bounded across the Rappahannock at Kelly's Ford, beat up the Confederate pickets there, and began an advance toward the Orange & Alexandria Railroad. Stuart and Pelham, who had taken a train to Culpeper, borrowed horses and rode toward the sound of the guns.

Pelham had no troops to command but, after arriving on the battlefield with Stuart, rode to the rear to find some good positions for artillery. Shortly he was back, before a stone fence where the Yankee cavalry had placed skirmishers. Pelham watched as the 3rd Virginia Cavalry in a column four abreast charged the Union skirmishers behind the stone fence, which was too high for their horses to leap. They turned left and rode along the fence yelling and firing at the Yankees behind it, looking for a gap in the fence or a gate near some farm buildings they were headed for.

Pelham drew his saber and cut diagonally toward the head of the column. The troops had found a gate at the farm buildings, and John Pelham rode up to it, standing in his stirrups, flourishing his saber over his head, smiling with boyish exuberance, and shouting, "Forward!"

In the melee and din, few heard the

☛ **W H A T · T O · S E E** Walking down the wood path, a visitor to the battle site can see part of the stone wall to the right, along which Union Cavalrymen posted themselves. A small stone monument replaced the wooden markers that for years identified the area where Pelham was mortally wounded. Closer to the Rappahannock River is the remnant of Strode's Mill, a pre-Revolutionary War mill that produced weapons for the Continental soldiers.

There are actually two Kelly's Fords. From the Route 620 bridge over the Rappahannock, ripples indicating a ford can be seen just upriver. According to research by Dr. John T. Dailey, who used Civil War-period illustrations, modern aerial photographs, and field triangulation, the Kelly's Ford used by the Union Cavalry is downriver from the bridge, at the visible downstream end of the island. The area is on private land and is posted "No Trespassing."

artillery shell burst overhead. Fewer still saw the handsome youngster fall from his horse. Those who did, saw him on his back, eyes open, the smile still on his lips. But he didn't move. The Yankees looked like they were gathering for a counterattack, and two officers lifted Pelham over the saddle of one of their horses. Perhaps then they noticed the tiny wound in the back of his skull at the hairline where a fragment of shell about the size of the tip of the little finger tore through him for two inches.

On the way to the rear it was noticed that he was still alive. The men procured an ambulance, and he was taken to the Shackleford home in Culpeper, where at 1:00 P.M. he opened his eyes, drew a long last breath, and died. ▪

GERMANNA FORD ON THE RAPIDAN

IT WAS A CROSSING OF A RIVER AS fateful and symbolic as Caesar's crossing of the Rubicon. In the damp, early morning hours on May 4, 1864, the veteran soldiers of the Army of the Potomac, with the resignation of journeymen waking for yet another weary day on the job, gathered in silence into their marching lines; the new recruits joked and laughed nervously. They slowly began the long

GERMANNA FORD CAN BE SEEN where Route 3, going west out of Fredericksburg, crosses the Rapidan.

march southward, which would be for all of them, one way or another, their last.

Between 2:00 and 3:00 A.M., cavalrymen from the 3rd Indiana cleared

☛ **W H A T · T O · S E E**   The general area around the old ford has been altered significantly by the recent expansion of Route 3 into a four-lane bridge across the Rapidan. The integrity of the ford area has been greatly compromised, but a walk around the area, especially on the south side of the Rapidan to west of the road, still reveals some old foundations and a chimney that seem to appear on illustrations done by Civil War artists. The northbound lane of Route 3 appears to run right over or very near to the pontoon bridge site, and most, if not all, Civil War remnants of the site have been obliterated by construction.

Confederates from Germanna Ford on the Rapidan River, while five miles downstream Union cavalry opened Ely's Ford for a second column of blue-coated infantry. Canvas and wooden pontoon bridges were laid by the engineers, and by 7:00 A.M. the Union Army Fifth Corps began to cross on the swaying, floating bridges at Germanna Ford. The Army of the Potomac would not cross this river again except in victory; many of the men of that army would be killed in the next day or two and would never cross it again at all.

Those men with a knowledge of history may have thought of the Rubicon; those with a religious bent probably imagined this was the River Styx. Watching them was the man who wouldn't let them go back until they won the war or died in the effort. Grant observed the crossing of his great army from the back of Cincinnati, his favorite mount. He was dressed uncharacteristically well, wearing his sash, sword, and even cotton gloves. Before long he would be back in his private's blouse. The procession he watched was indeed historic; the men crossing at Germanna and Ely's fords would win the war. ∎

ELY'S FORD ON THE RAPIDAN

ELY'S FORD, LIKE GERMANNA FORD, played a role in the Fredericksburg and Chancellorsville campaigns. Cavalry guarded both of them, and infantry used them as crossing points, but as with Germanna Ford, Ely's most historic moment came when Maj. Gen. Winfield Scott Hancock's Second Corps of the Union Army crossed there on May 4, 1864, as part of Grant's movement south.

The most notable feature of Ely's Ford to the individual infantryman was the steep hill on its south side. The road over Ely's Ford led more directly to the old battleground of Chancel-

ELY'S FORD CAN BE REACHED from the battlefield of Chancellorsville by following Route 610 northwest off of Route 3.

lorsville, and the men of Hancock's Second Corps encamped upon the former field of strife among the scattered skeletons of soldiers gone before them: Human skulls and bones were everywhere, and many of the living contemplated, like Hamlet, the last, earthbound relics of those once so much like them. ∎

FREDERICKSBURG: 1862

THE TERRAIN AROUND AND TO THE west of Fredericksburg, Virginia, is cut by numerous small rivers that drain the red clay soil and eventually end up feeding either the Rappahannock or the York River farther to the south. Some of the rivers, like the Ni, the Po, or Massaponax Creek, after heavy rain can be substantial enough to affect military tactics, and certainly the larger rivers like the Rapidan and the Rappahannock and their fords had a marked effect upon three major campaigns through the area.

If you could have looked at the city of Fredericksburg, Virginia, from one of Professor Thaddeus Lowe's hydrogen balloons in 1862, you would have realized that it is really only half a city. As in many waterfront communities, some streets seem to go for blocks, then abruptly end as if dropping off into the water. Some of these streets don't end at the water, however, but as trace roads seem to descend right into the Rappahannock. Some of

FREDERICKSBURG, VIRGINIA, can be reached from the north or south via several exits from I-95, and from the southeast or northwest by following U.S. Route 17. Virginia state Route 3 runs through Fredericksburg from east to west.

these are the sites of the Union pontoon bridges laid to facilitate the crossing (and eventual recrossing) of the river during the horrible conflict in December 1862 known as the Battle of Fredericksburg.

The river, at what is referred to as the middle pontoon crossing at the southern end of the town of Fredericksburg, is about fourteen feet deep—enough to allow the passage of some smaller classes of gunboats of the Union Navy that drew between six and ten feet of water. In fact, the crossing where the middle pontoon bridge was laid was referred to by Union commander General Burnside as a steamboat landing.[4] No Union gunboats were brought this far up the Rappahannock, however. The Union Navy tried, but Confederate general Daniel Harvey Hill stopped them downriver at Port Royal. The river at the middle pontoon crossing is narrow—not even one hundred yards wide in some spots, with the channel narrower than that—and would become a bottleneck for any more than one or two of the gunboats, which despite their shallow draft were sometimes two hundred feet long.

While support from the Union Navy was not feasible at the upper end of the Rappahannock River, the use of another type of boat was essential for the Union Army to engage in battle at Fredericksburg in the winter of 1862.

By mid-November, with the Confederate Army of Northern Virginia on the Fredericksburg side of the Rappahannock and Burnside's Union Army on the opposite side, the entire operation for the Federals depended upon the successful crossing of the river. Burnside had ordered pontoon bridges to be brought to the army as he quickly moved his huge force of 110,000 men to Falmouth, Virginia, across the Rappahannock from Fredericksburg. But the wagons carrying the disassembled pontoon bridges arrived a week after his army did and

gave Robert E. Lee and his army, with about 78,000 troops, time to establish a well-entrenched position. By this late date in the war, Lee's men were exquisitely skilled in the art of field fortifications.

Yet even after the pontoons were available to the Federal Army, Lee still wasn't certain where to expect the main Union attack. His lines were nearly seven miles long, anchored on the left at a large hill known as Marye's Heights, which overlooked the town of Fredericksburg, and stretching down the Rappahannock to end at Hamilton's Railroad Crossing. The Union Army was stretched at least that far and could theoretically cross the Rappahannock above or below the Confederate lines, where the crossing could be unopposed.

In fact, Burnside had determined to cross the river at Skinker's Neck, some fourteen miles below Fredericksburg; then, in some convoluted thought process, he decided that after all the activity there, the place Lee would least expect him to cross was at Fredericksburg itself.[5] The plan was to throw pontoon bridges about one and one-quarter miles below the city and three more across the Rappahannock at Fredericksburg: two at the northern end and one more at the southern end of the town.

Whether he was correct at out-

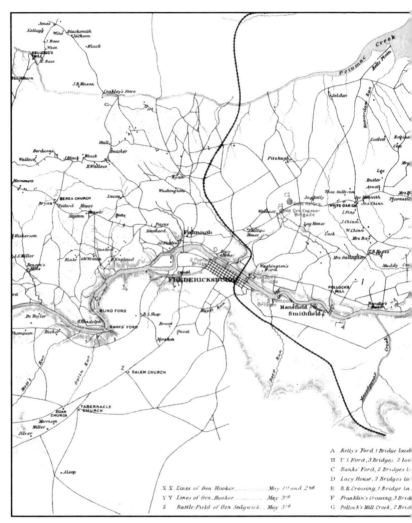

The Battle of Fredericksburg

guessing Lee didn't matter for long, because on the foggy morning of December 11, 1862, as the pontoon bridge builders were about halfway across the river, the fog lifted slightly, and they were exposed to concentrated fire from a small group of Mississippi riflemen lodged in rifle pits and in some of the houses along the river's edge.

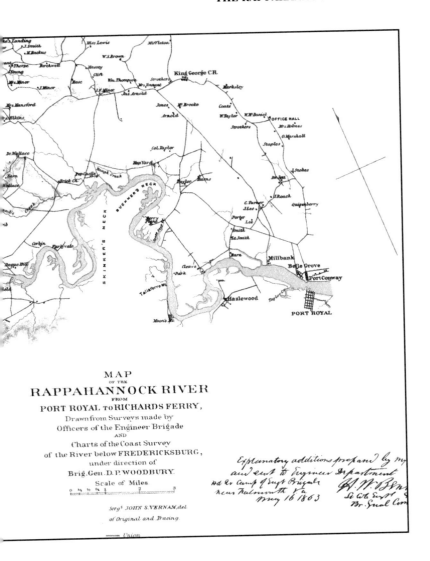

MAP
OF THE
RAPPAHANNOCK RIVER
FROM
PORT ROYAL TO RICHARDS FERRY,
Drawn from Surveys made by
Officers of the Engineer Brigade
AND
Charts of the Coast Survey
of the River below FREDERICKSBURG,
under direction of
Brig.Gen.D.P.WOODBURY.
Scale of Miles

Serg¹ JOHN S.VERNAM.del
of Original and Tracing

At least nine separate attempts were made by the Union engineers and their crews to construct the pontoon bridges, from dawn until about 10:00 A.M. Each was forced to halt by the stinging fire of the men from the 17th Mississippi, some sharpshooters from the 13th Mississippi, and three companies of the 18th Mississippi Infantry.

The Federals called their heavy

artillery on Stafford Heights into action to bombard the town and drive the Confederates from their positions. Under cover of the tremendous barrage, the engineer units attempted to finish their bridges, but for the artillerists behind and above them it was like trying to hit a swarm of mosquitoes with a baseball bat, and the Federals on the bridges still fell from the fire of the Mississippians.[6]

Finally at 4:30 P.M., as the December sun began to set and Lee had realized where Burnside intended to cross his army, volunteers from the 7th Michigan Infantry and the 89th New York Infantry climbed into some of the pontoons. The term "amphibi-

---

☛ **W H A T · T O · S E E** Tours of Fredericksburg and the battlefields around the town itself are recommended. The National Park Service offers a self-guided auto tour of the four major battlefields (Fredericksburg, Chancellorsville, the Wilderness, and Spotsylvania) in a brochure from the Visitor Center near the National Cemetery on Marye's Heights (follow the signs). Some Civil War sites you should not miss are the Upper and Middle Pontoon Crossing Sites; Chatham Mansion (across the Rappahannock from Fredericksburg); the Confederate Cemetery; the Slave Auction Block, a stark, cold reminder of a civilization built upon human bondage and brought down by it; and lovely Brompton Mansion (not open to the public, but it can be viewed from the Sunken Road), nearly destroyed by the two battles for Marye's Heights and later used as a hospital. From the National Park Service Visitor Center you can obtain information on both driving and walking tours of the town.

Additional information is available from the Fredericksburg Visitor Center, Box FB, 706 Caroline Street, Fredericksburg, VA 22401. In addition to Civil War battlefields, Fredericksburg boasts many Colonial and Revolutionary Period sites, so you may want to stay a few days. There are numerous fine restaurants, and overnight accommodations are abundant.

Though the Rappahannock River is navigable to the middle pontoon bridge site, there is no place for even a temporary tie-up. The city of Fredericksburg maintains a small, two-ramp dock with a large parking area. The area is patrolled by police, and if you contact the authorities, you may be able to launch and leave your trailer and tow vehicle overnight if you intend to cruise downriver for an overnighter to Tappahannock or Urbanna.

ous assault" probably would have drawn blank stares from the officers and men piling into the pontoons. Yet that is exactly what they were doing—conducting an amphibious assault across an open body of water, exposed to fire from the opposite bank, making an effort to land and drive off the defenders. It was one of several times during the Civil War that this tactic was used.

After driving the sharpshooting Mississippians from the water's edge, the Union assault troops secured the bridgeheads, and construction continued on the bridges. The following day the rest of their army crossed the Rappahannock. More than 1,200 of them were killed in the fighting the next day.

On December 13, Union assaults rolled out like blue waves disintegrating in a crimson mist from the town of Fredericksburg toward a Confederate line four deep, well concealed along a sunken road and stone fence. No Union soldier got within forty yards of the position, but Burnside continued to order assault after assault. As the waves receded, they left human beings like effluvium on a beach, to be picked up and dumped unceremoniously into graves chopped from the frozen Virginia loam.

For another 11,000 wounded Union soldiers, the recrossing of the Rappahannock after the battle would be the beginning of a painful journey toward possible recovery, or an agonizing demise resulting from primitive surgical techniques and infection. ▪

PORT ROYAL

PORT ROYAL ON THE RAPPAHANNOCK River was established in 1744 as one of the more important colonial ports on the Rappahannock. In 1862 Burnside thought about crossing the river here on his Fredericksburg Campaign. Confederate general D. H. Hill in December 1862 drove back a contingent of Union gunboats as they attempted to steam upriver to support Burnside's movement to Fredericksburg.

PORT ROYAL IS JUST OFF OF U.S. Route 301 on the south side of the Rappahannock where 301 crosses the river. Boaters can find Port Royal as they reach buoys marked in the mid-70s. (Buoy "75 Fl G 4sec 12ft" appears to be the last one downstream from the Route 301 bridge at Port Tobacco.) There are no public tie-up facilities.

Because of Grant's whirlwind campaign from the Rapidan River through Virginia to the James, Port Royal on the Rappahannock served as Grant's base of supplies for only four days. In fact, Grant went through four bases of supplies from May 10, when he established one at Belle Plain until June 22, when City Point became his base of supplies through the end of the war.

One can imagine the frustration of Grant's engineers as they laid pontoon wharves on Potomac Creek at Belle Plain on May 9–10, moved between May 22 and May 26 to Port Royal on the Rappahannock; moved again on May 30 to establish a base of supplies by June 5 at White House on the Pamunkey; then finally switched to City Point by June 22. ∎

☞ **W H A T · T O · S E E** Port Royal is one of the quaint but little visited towns in this part of Virginia. Some of the houses are obviously of colonial provenance. The Robert Gilchrist House, right on the edge of the river, with its wooden shake shingles and tall, floor-length windows, was obviously here during the town's era of Civil War importance, having been built around 1750.

Across the river from Port Royal is Port Conway, where on the morning of April 24, 1865, Lincoln's assassin, John Wilkes Booth, crossed the Rappahannock to Port Royal in his efforts to escape. He continued two and one-half miles down what is now Route 301 to a farmhouse owned by a Mr. Garrett. He hid out in Garrett's tobacco barn, where he was shot and killed by a Union cavalryman named Boston Corbett. The Garrett farmhouse site is now within the confines of Fort A. P. Hill.

The pontoon wharf at Port Royal was anchored about where the newly constructed Route 301 bridge now crosses the Rappahannock.[7]

URBANNA ON THE LOWER RAPPAHANNOCK: 1862

BEGINNING IN JANUARY 1862, GEN. George McClellan seemed fixated with a plan to launch a campaign against Richmond using the little town of Urbanna on the Rappahannock River as his base of supplies.

McClellan's plan to use the Chesapeake Bay and the rivers flowing across Virginia into the bay as highways for men and matériel was a sound one in the beginning. Until the Confederates had the capabilities to blockade the rivers by mining them (with "torpedoes," as Civil War–era underwater mines were called) or until they had a naval force that could threaten to sink one or more of the large transports loaded to the gunwales with men, McClellan was on the right track.

He submitted to Lincoln and his superiors what came to be known as "The Urbanna Plan." Urbanna, Virginia, is located at the mouth of the Rappahannock River only about fifty miles overland from Richmond. McClellan's Urbanna Plan was to land a force there and rapidly march the fifty miles to Richmond, using Urbanna on the Rappahannock and West Point on the York River as bases of waterborne supply, before Gen. Joseph E. Johnston and his Confederate Army, entrenched around

URBANNA, VIRGINIA, CAN BE reached from U.S. Route 17 southeast of Fredericksburg. From Route 17, take Route 602 to Urbanna. For those who wish to boat to Urbanna, the town has several marinas located on Urbanna Creek. Inquiries can be made for information from the Urbanna Chamber of Commerce, Drawer C, Urbanna, VA 23175, telephone (804) 758-5540.

Manassas (near Washington), could reach the capital of the Confederacy to defend it.

Lincoln disagreed. He wanted McClellan to advance toward Manassas and fight the Confederate forces there. The major difference between the two strategies was that McClellan's objective was the capture of Richmond, while Lincoln's objective was to defeat the Confederate Army. This obsession Union commanders had with capturing Richmond, rather than with finding and fighting the Confederate Army, would be a major misunderstanding between Lincoln and all his generals until U. S. Grant came east in the spring of 1864.

Lincoln finally approved McClellan's plan, but the Confederates at Manassas under Johnston were not going to cooperate. Apparently, McClellan thought they would just sit still at Manassas until he completed his planning, organized and reorganized his army, built up its strength, and transported it to the gates of Richmond. On March 9, 1862, with word of the Confederate ironclad *Merrimack's* rampage in Hampton Roads creating a near panic in Washington, and Lincoln and his cabinet expecting to see the menacing ironclad steaming up the Potomac at any moment, some strange telegrams began arriving from the field: Confederates were withdrawing from their fortified lines along the upper and lower Potomac. Stranger still, Johnston had evacuated his lines at Manassas and had withdrawn his army toward Richmond.

Suddenly, after all the time spent planning and worrying, McClellan was ready to move boldly. In full battle array, the entire Union Army of 112,000, with McClellan leading, advanced upon Manassas. If the news of abandoned Confederate lines had finally given McClellan the resolve to advance grandly, the fact that many of the heavy artillery pieces observed in the Confederate trenches were found to be only painted logs gave the newspapers and photographers fodder for ridiculing his months of delay in advancing to battle. The landing at

---

☛ **WHAT · TO · SEE** But for the fortunes of war, Urbanna might have become, if only for a short while, one of the busiest ports in the world, catering to the needs of and funneling the supplies for more than 100,000 Union soldiers. As it turned out, Urbanna today is a small town (permanent population about 500) tuned to the seasons when tourists flood the rental cottages and when the local watermen pull crabs, fish, and oysters from the river. Several historic sites remain in town.

Urbanna was originally an early trading port, then tobacco became the main product to be shipped out. The Association for the Preservation of Virginia Antiquities has restored the old Tobacco Warehouse (ca. 1766) on Virginia Street. Across Virginia Street is a privately owned residence once used as a customs house as early as 1680. Farther up Virginia Street is the Old Court House, of particular interest to Civil War enthusiasts, as it once housed Confederate troops. Also up Virginia Street is Lansdowne, the home to which Arthur Lee, kinsman of Confederate general Robert E. Lee, retired.

Urbanna with the objective of getting between Richmond and the Confederate Army at Manassas was now impossible. McClellan changed his plan: He would land his army at the Union stronghold of Fort Monroe and advance up the Virginia Peninsula between the York and James rivers and take Richmond that way. ▪

Notes

1. Grant, Vol. II, 179–80.
2. Freeman, Vol. II, 350.
3. *Historic Culpeper*, 148.
4. Maj. Gen. Ambrose Burnside's report, *Official Records of the War of the Rebellion*, Vol. XXI, 87–89.
5. *Ibid.*
6. Maj. Gen. Lafayette McLaws, "The Confederate Left at Fredericksburg," *Battles and Leaders of the Civil War*, Vol. III, 87.
7. Frassanito, *Grant and Lee*, 152.

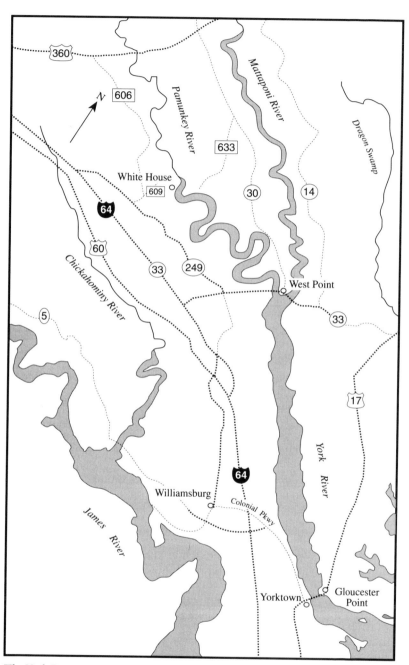

The York River

✦ THE YORK RIVER ✦

GLOUCESTER POINT

THE YORK RIVER, FROM WEST POINT where the Pamunkey and Mattaponi join, for nearly twenty-six statute miles to Gloucester Point across from the old Colonial town of Yorktown, averages between two and one-half and three miles in width, with a channel from one-half to one mile wide. But at Gloucester Point the river narrows to one-half mile. Because of this, the Confederates early in the war dug extensive earthworks, improving, in some cases, upon British-made works built eighty years before during the Siege of Yorktown in 1781. These earthworks include a partially completed star fort. The Confederates placed some of their largest artillery pieces at Gloucester Point. Between Confederate artillery in Yorktown and on Gloucester Point, a killing crossfire could be laid down against any Union ships attempting to ascend the York.

But neither the Confederates nor the British were the first to see the advantages of fortifications at this narrow spot in the York River. Originally mapped by Robert Tindall in 1608, Gloucester Point bore his name for

GLOUCESTER POINT CAN BE reached by following U.S. Route 17 from Fredericksburg southeast through the town of Gloucester or by crossing the Route 17 bridge from Yorktown north to Gloucester Point. For those who wish to boat to Gloucester, a highly recommended marina is the York River Yacht Haven on Sarah Creek directly across from Yorktown. The marina is only about a mile downstream from the Route 17 bridge and will arrange transportation to Yorktown and other points.

many years, and in 1667 the Virginia general assembly ordered a fort built at Tindall's Point to protect ships docking for trade. In 1676, after Bacon's rebellion, Virginia governor Sir William Berkeley held court-martials aboard a ship anchored off the point.[1]

The Siege of Yorktown in 1781 brought renewed activity at Gloucester Point. During the spring and summer of 1781, British commander Earl

65

Lord Cornwallis, fighting off the pursuing Continental forces under the Marquis de LaFayette and Anthony Wayne, moved eastward on the Virginia Peninsula between the York and James rivers. Cornwallis chose Yorktown as the place he felt he could defend while protecting the anchorage for the British supply ships he would need for further campaigning. His mistake was that Yorktown lay eleven miles up the York River, and any fleet controlling the Chesapeake Bay would also control waterborne supplies to the British Army. During the late summer and early fall, allied American and French forces from both land and sea converged upon the bottleneck between Yorktown and Gloucester Point.

By mid-September, the Continental troops of LaFayette and Wayne were joined by the combined armies of Gen. George Washington and Count de Rochambeau, who had marched from New York after hearing of the French fleet's approach toward Chesapeake Bay. When Washington arrived at Williamsburg on the Virginia Peninsula, he learned of the French fleet's defeat of the British ships sent to destroy the French transports carrying Washington's siege guns to Yorktown. The British, instead of destroying the Americans' ability for laying siege to Yorktown, sailed on to New York. With them went Cornwallis's ability to supply his army by sea.

Cornwallis had sent a force across the York from Yorktown to Gloucester Point. There they built, according to one historian, four redoubts, a line of entrenchments across the tip of the Point, and emplaced nineteen guns.[2]

French artillery drove one British ship, the frigate *Guadeloupe*, from a supporting position in the York River to the shore near Gloucester Point, where it burned and sank. As well, the British ship *Charon* was set afire by hot shot from the French battery and sank.[3] The two ships joined thirteen others scuttled in the York River by Cornwallis when he got word of the French fleet's dominating presence in Chesapeake Bay. Cornwallis had removed the heavy artillery from the ships first and had emplaced them in his works at Yorktown. Many of the guns were served by seamen displaced by necessity from their ships. The remains of the British ships lie today in a semicircle just offshore Yorktown in about seventy-five feet of water, having felt the vibrations of ships passing above for two centuries change from steam-powered Civil War vessels to rumbling diesel engines of World War II warships to the modern gasoline engines of recreational powerboats. The area is now protected, listed on the National Register of Historic Places.[4]

Once the French Fleet secured the Chesapeake Bay, it became obvious to everyone, including Lord Cornwallis, who had been living in a cave at the edge of the river bluff for a week, that not only would there be no resupply, but there would be no escape either. At 10:00 that morning, the British sent out a flag of truce. Terms were discussed, and the surrender of the British garrison at Gloucester and Yorktown was effected on October 19, 1781.

The trenches and fortifications at Gloucester Point and across the river at Yorktown would weather and soften under the Virginia rains for a generation, until they were manned again in another war against the British, the War of 1812. Forty-nine years later the sites would be improved upon and occupied by troops during the Civil War, the passage of nearly two centuries from its first fort in 1667 having had no effect whatsoever upon the tactical significance of Gloucester Point.

Maps made by Union engineers on May 4–6, 1862, after the Confederates abandoned their positions show the details of the forts both on Gloucester Point and within Yorktown itself. The star fort on Gloucester Point was actually more rectangular than circular, looking much like a turtle heading away from the Point. It had eight-foot-high walls and an eight-foot-deep ditch around it. The walls were between thirteen and twenty feet thick. The fort was designed to mount at least thirteen guns, including two rifled pieces. In front of and below the fort was a "water battery," placed there to lay down a more horizontal fire closer to any ships trying to run the gauntlet. It, in turn, would be protected by the star fort's large guns lobbing shells over it. ▪

☛ **W H A T · T O · S E E** Development has compromised nearly all of the massive star fort on Gloucester Point: The Route 17 bridge runs right through the site of the fort. Only a small percentage of one of the original redoubts (smaller field fortifications constructed in advance) of the fort still remains and can be seen to the west (the upstream side) of Route 17 just before reaching the bridge to cross to Yorktown.

YORKTOWN

YORKTOWN, SITE OF THE AMERICAN and French siege against the British in the Revolutionary War, was by the spring of 1862 again surrounded by high earthworks. According to Lieutenant Comstock, who worked on the drawings of the abandoned Confederate fortifications in early May 1862, they contained no less than twenty-seven large guns facing the river, including eight-inch Columbiads, nine- and ten-inch Dahlgrens, and some rifled thirty-two pounders. There were five furnaces for hot shot (heated projectiles fired against the sails and rigging of enemy ships to set them on fire) and some twenty-six more guns facing down the peninsula where Union troops would advance. Outer works to slow up siege operations were in place, and a series of traverses south of the earthworks were also noted on Comstock's drawings. Confederates dug in behind the Warwick River, which ran from near the Yorktown fortifications all the way across the peninsula. They used the swampy areas and the river as a natural impediment for troops advancing against their lines.[5]

As long as Gloucester Point and Yorktown remained in Confederate hands, any Union advance up the peninsula would have its right flank unprotected and vulnerable to any

> TO REACH YORKTOWN FROM Williamsburg, follow the Colonial Parkway along the York River. Signs in Williamsburg will direct you to the Parkway. Yorktown is also accessible from the south via U.S. Route 17. Follow signs to the historic sites.

number of types of attacks—a full-scale bombardment by Confederate gunboats on the York River, a rebel infantry assault protected by southern gunboats, or Confederate infantry or cavalry landed behind the Union lines by ships. Clearly, Union general George B. McClellan, after his successful amphibious landing at Fort Monroe in the spring of 1862, still needed to drive the Confederates from their positions at Yorktown in order to proceed with his plans to advance upon Richmond.

April 5, 1862, to May 4, 1862

Using the Warwick River as a natural obstacle in front of his works and marching his men to show themselves at different points in his fortifications, Confederate general John B. Magruder gave McClellan the impression that he strongly held a formidable position in and around the old Revolutionary War fortifications at Yorktown. From

April 5, 1862, McClellan began building field fortifications to contain and protect the massive siege guns needed to bombard Yorktown into submission. For a month his men were stationary in their lines, working diligently each day as laborers instead of soldiers, their commanding general believing each report of the ever-growing numbers of rebels rushing to defend Yorktown. Suddenly, on May 4, the report came in to McClellan that no rebel sentries could be seen. After all McClellan's work preparing for a siege, Confederate general Joseph E. Johnston, who had taken over command from Magruder, had pulled his men out of their works at Yorktown and retreated up the peninsula.

Fighting a rearguard action at Williamsburg, the old colonial capital, Johnston withdrew his army to the gates of Richmond and McClellan cautiously followed. The scene was set for the summer campaign on the peninsula, which would see McClellan and his great northern host driven from the close environs of the Confederate capital back to his bases on the James and the emergence, after the wounding of Johnston, of another Confederate general whose fame would outshine all others and live imperishable in American history—Robert E. Lee.

Detailed descriptions of the fighting around Richmond and the Seven

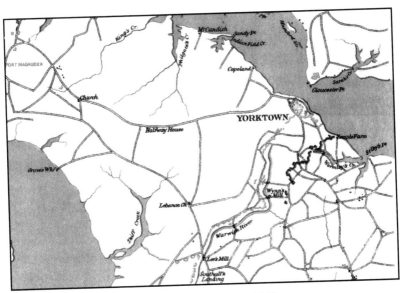

Confederate defensive works at Yorktown in May 1862

☛ **W H A T · T O · S E E** The significance of Yorktown's role in the Civil War is overshadowed by the role the town played at the climax of the American Revolution. References on the battlefield to the 1862 Peninsula Campaign are fairly rare, as its history is interpreted to the public to reflect its importance to colonial America and American independence. The situation at Yorktown is certainly a preservationist's conundrum: Early Revolutionary War–era earthworks were altered by Civil War–era fortifications, which themselves became historic. Immediately following the siege, Washington had the Allied army's earthworks destroyed so they couldn't be used again. In the 1930s, the National Park Service reconstructed the Allied siegelines. For the visitor, the question becomes, Which era earthworks am I looking at? The answer, of course, is both, and yet they have been altered as well by efforts of the National Park Service and by the passing of time.

Other sites to see are the several eighteenth-century buildings that survived both sieges of Yorktown. The Nelson House and the Moore House, which appears in some Civil War photographs, are both restored and open to the public. Some of the other historic houses are privately owned and not open to the public. A self-guided walking tour of Yorktown is available and encouraged. The town retains much of its colonial-era ambience, and the walking tour (or just parts of it, since it is rather extensive) is the perfect way to see it. On the tour you'll pass several restored eighteenth-century buildings, including the reconstructed Swan Tavern Group, the original buildings of which were destroyed by an explosion of ammunition during the Civil War. Cornwallis's Cave, where he spent much of the siege, is on the tour, as is the Watermen's Museum, interpreting the role of one of Virginia's most enduring industries, and the Yorktown Victory Center, where reenactors portray the lives of soldiers in a Continental Army camp.

Information on the self-guided walking tour is available from the York County Information Office, P.O. Box 532, Yorktown, VA 23690, telephone (804) 890-3300. The Yorktown Victory Center is also a source for information at P.O. Box 1776, Yorktown, VA 23690, telephone (804) 887-1776. For historical inquiries, contact the National Park Service at Colonial National Historical Park, P.O. Box 210, Yorktown, VA 23690, telephone (804) 898-3400.

Days Battles until the Union Army was driven back to the James River are not within the scope of this book. It is recommended, however, that anyone visiting the area of the peninsula also visit Richmond National Battlefield Park and the battle sites on the tour offered there. In "The James River: 1864" chapter, the discussion of the Bermuda Hundred Campaign will include descriptions of some of the fighting on the other side of the James. ∎

WHITE HOUSE ON THE PAMUNKEY

WHITE HOUSE LANDING WAS MC-Clellan's original base of supplies in his Peninsula Campaign in the spring of 1862. On navigable waters (the Pamunkey River channel is between nine and twenty-nine feet deep there), White House Landing could be connected to main bases of supplies up the Potomac via the York River, into which it emptied. A railroad connected White House Landing with West Point, located at the confluence where the Pamunkey and Mattaponi formed the York, then ran in the opposite direction from White House Landing to Richmond. The old, white dwelling house, from which the landing got its name, held historical and emotional memories for the Civil War soldiers, both Union and Confederate.

Local history has it that it was to White House that the guests at the wedding of its owner, Martha Custis, and her new husband, George Washington, came for their reception in 1759. The property passed down

THE PAMUNKEY HAS NUMEROUS turns and loops, and by water from West Point, White House Landing appears to be about twenty-nine statute miles. A launch ramp is shown about four miles downriver from the landing where Route 633 (leading south off Route 30) ends at the Pamunkey, but much shoaling is indicated within a mile of the put-in. White House Landing is just downstream from the modern railroad bridge marked on charts "swing bridge hor cl draw 53 ft vert cl 4 ft." According to historian William Frassanito, remains of barges burned and sunk during McClellan's evacuation can still be seen in the area at low tide.[6] (Note: This information is not for navigational purposes. Always consult current NOS charts and documents, Local Notices to Mariners, and local boaters before planning a cruise.)

through the Washington-Custis generations until one William Henry Fitzhugh Lee inherited it and made his home there. W. H. F. Lee, also called "Rooney," was the son of Mary Anne Randolph Custis and Gen. Robert E. Lee and became a Confederate general himself, commanding troops under Gen. Jeb Stuart.

During the spring of 1862, McClellan slowly moved up the Virginia Peninsula between the York and the James after he had seen the Confederates abandon Yorktown and had pushed them out of Williamsburg. By May 15 he had established twin bases of supplies at West Point, where the Mattaponi and Pamunkey merge to form the York, and at White House Landing above West Point on the Pamunkey, which was connected to West Point both by water and by rail.

According to at least one historian, McClellan, by using the York River ports as bases of supply, backed himself into two tactical corners. First, to get to Richmond, he would have to cross his army over the Chickahominy River—which splits the peninsula between Richmond and the Pamunkey—and yet leave a good portion of his army north of it to guard his bases and his supply lines. The Chickahominy drains numerous swampy areas east of Richmond and was susceptible to flooding during inclement weather. A rise in the river would split his army in two. Second, McClellan sadly overestimated the railroad that ran from West Point through White House and on to Richmond. It was merely a single track and was also prone to flooding and destruction in sections by the heavy rains that frequently fall in the area. With two large rivers and a railroad for supplies, the army was still dependent upon wagon trains for its main source of supply.[7]

On May 30, 1862, a violent, rain-filled storm front moved into the peninsula area of Virginia, swelling the Chickahominy four feet above its average depth and turning it into a swift, dangerous river. Dirt and corduroy roads and log bridges disappeared before the soldiers' eyes. Because of the rain and impassability of the Chickahominy, Confederate general Joseph E. Johnston launched an all-out attack upon McClellan at a place called Seven Pines. Two days of battle produced a draw, and McClellan continued—as he had done since his appointment as head of the army—to petition Lincoln for more and more troops. For the next week the rain continued, stalling both armies in their tracks.

But even when the rains ended and the roads dried, McClellan still hesitated. While he procrastinated, Robert E. Lee, given command of the Confederate army after Joseph Johnston's wounding at Seven Pines, used the time to reorganize, dig defensive works around part of Richmond, and send his young cavalry leader, Jeb Stuart, on a foray behind McClellan's lines to gather information on the enemy.

Stuart left the main Confederate lines on June 12, 1862, and before his ride was over had swept to within a few miles of White House in the rear of the Union lines, cutting communications between the Union Army and their main base of supplies. Stuart had probably thought of attacking the enemy's base at White House, but knowing that it was protected by a large guard and by gunboats on the river, he turned away. Riding with him was the owner of the estate at White House, Col. W. H. F. Lee.

Stuart's ride completely around the enemy army provided Lee with the information he needed. More than that, it boosted the Confederates' morale, both in the field and on the home front, and made a folk hero out of Jeb Stuart. What it did to McClellan was more substantial. He began to remove much of his troop strength from north of the Chickahominy, leaving just one corps to guard White House and his lines of supply and communications. In addition, he ordered a huge standing supply of rations moved from the depot at White House to the James.[8] It seemed

as if he were finally realizing that his advance should have been based upon the James River to begin with. Or perhaps the overly cautious McClellan was already defeated in his own mind and was preparing to abandon his positions north of the Chickahominy.

On June 25 the string of fights began that have come to be called the Seven Days' Battles. Already, by June 26, Lee was threatening the Union Army's base at White House and McClellan was preparing to change his base of supplies some thirty miles south to Harrison's Landing on the James. In the early morning hours of June 27, the dangerous and ponderous job of moving virtually an entire city on four hundred ships and on overland routes was begun. Over two thousand head of cattle were driven from White House Landing toward the James and supplies were loaded upon the ships with the millions of cartridges and artillery ammunition given priority. The railroad cars that could not be shipped were burned, along with any supplies that were left behind. Immense stores of equipment, food, weapons, ammunition, reserve artillery, beef on the hoof, communications equipment, and wagons filled to the brim began the arduous crossing of the Virginia Peninsula, replete with mud, rivers, swamps . . . and the enemy.

The rising smoke coming from the

White House Landing on June 27 and the lurid light emanating from the area all night no doubt filled Rooney Lee with apprehension. When the cavalry finally arrived at White House, Lee discovered that the magnificent house had been burned to the ground. Though some historians like to point out that the original historic White House had been burned thirty years before,[9] that knowledge could have been of little consolation to the son of the commanding general as he came upon the smoldering ruins of his home.

Rooney Lee's personal tragedy would grow even deeper before the war ended. Wounded at Brandy Station in June 1863, he was captured—taken from his sickbed—by Union soldiers and incarcerated, first at Fort Monroe at Old Point Comfort, then at Johnson's Island in Lake Erie. While he was a prisoner, the Union Army considered hanging him in retaliation for the threatened execution of some Union officers. His wife, the frail and delicate Charlotte Wickham Lee, was affected by the strain, lost her health, and died at Christmas 1863. Folk history relates that she breathed her last calling for her dear husband and that the Yankee Secretary of War had a hand in disallowing the noble, humane thing, which would have been to allow Lee to visit his dying wife one last time.[10] Fact or fable, this is one of the many reasons why enmity ran bitter through the hearts of Southerners for generations after the war.

White House Landing in 1864

Send Butler's forces to White House, to land on the north side, and march up to join this army. . . .
        —U. S. Grant, May 25, 1864

Even before Ulysses Grant's base of supplies at Port Royal on the Rappahannock was fully operational, he was already sending troops through his soon-to-be base of supplies at White House Landing on the Pamunkey River. By the end of May 1864 he would be in the process of switching bases, and by June 5 his base at White House Landing was established. Grant was going through bases of supply one after another as his army continued to

---

☛ **W H A T · T O · S E E** The old White House estate is privately owned today and inaccessible to the public except by permission. The Pamunkey is navigable, but shoaling is indicated in random areas, and there are no maintained daymarks indicated above West Point.

sidestep Lee and slip farther south. After the Battle of the Wilderness and the fighting around Spotsylvania and on the North Anna, Grant turned the head of his army southeastward and had to shift his base of supplies from Belle Plain on Potomac Creek on May 22 to Port Royal on the Rappahannock by May 26. Once Grant crossed the Pamunkey River in his inexorable drive around Lee's right flank, he was able to establish his base of supplies by June 5 at White House on the Pamunkey.

He wasn't over yet. Driving and fighting through some of the old battlegrounds of McClellan's 1862 campaign, and fighting his own horrifyingly costly battle at Cold Harbor, he would finally switch his base of supplies to City Point by June 22, after he had slipped across the James River on the night of June 14. Though the bases changed enough to keep his engineers working overtime, the supply centers all had one thing in common: They were located on the waterfront of a major river. ▪

Notes

1. *Virginia: A Guide to the Old Dominion*, 458–59.
2. Scheer and Rankin, 555.
3. Selby, 190–91.
4. James Haskett, chief historian, Colonial National Historical Park, telephone interview with the author, December 18, 1992.
5. *Atlas to Accompany the Official Records of the Union and Confederate Armies*, plates XV, XVII, XIX.
6. Frassanito, *Grant and Lee*, 168.
7. Cullen, 52.
8. *Ibid.*, 78.
9. Freeman, Vol. 1, 634n.
10. Thomason, 411.

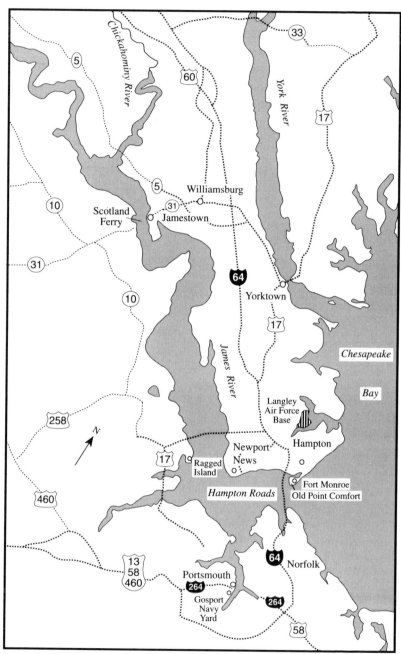

The Lower James River

✦ THE JAMES RIVER: 1862 ✦

PERHAPS, OF ALL THE rivers in America, only the Mississippi is as historic as the James. Archaeologists have found artifacts on the banks of the James dating back some eleven thousand years; pottery shards and tobacco pipes, glass beads and leather pieces, remains of Native American dwelling houses and weapon points all have been found near enough to the great river to indicate that it was a vital part of the ancient inhabitants' lives. One wonders just what the James has pulled to itself and washed away over the millennia.

The English Colonial Period, though nearly four hundred years past, is the relatively recent era of history in the James River/Tidewater area of Virginia. Yet the river as an avenue to Jamestown and that village's significance as the first permanent English settlement in North America is unsurpassed in importance by all the waterborne immigrations to America in the four centuries since. It was the first of many to come.

During the American Civil War, the peninsula between the James River to the south and the York River to the north was one of the most fought-over, marched-across, and camped-in areas in America. As a native Virginian once said, you can't throw a bucket of water out a window in Tidewater Virginia without getting some historic site wet.

The first major battle of the Civil War was fought at Big Bethel—now part of Langley Air Force Base—on June 10, 1861, as Federal forces advanced from Fort Monroe. Fort Monroe, which remained in Federal hands the entire war, became the stepping-off point for a number of Union amphibious invasions of the Confederacy and subsequent overland marches toward Richmond. Norfolk and the adjacent Gosport Navy Yard in Portsmouth were abandoned, then eventually reoccupied by U.S. forces. Hampton Roads was the scene of the first battle between ironclad warships in America. Another result of the Federal victory was the Union's *Monitor* remaining in the James. The ship's intimidating presence would have more of an effect on the outcome of the war than the victory itself. Hampton Roads was also the site of one of the first submarine attacks upon a surface vessel.

Fighting—from great battles to small skirmishes—occurred on the peninsula throughout the war, but the two years that the armies were most active there were 1862, during the spring and summer when Union general George McClellan tried to use the peninsula as a broad thoroughfare to Richmond, and 1864, when Ulysses S. Grant fought and moved across it on his way to maneuvering around Gen. Robert E. Lee and the Confederate Army.

During the war, the James River was denied to the Confederacy and secured for the Union as a supply route both strategically by the Union blockade and, more importantly, tactically by the Federal James River gunboat flotilla. Had the Confederacy been able to keep this as well as the other rivers open, their supply routes from the Southern ports, or even the flow of supplies from elsewhere on the river, could have remained open. They wouldn't have had to rely completely on vulnerable overland routes for ammunition, food, and other supplies. The James River was the great waterway that potentially could supply any army in eastern Virginia indefinitely. Only the Union Army made this potential a reality.

As the war progressed and Grant made his headquarters and base of supplies on the James, then began operations both north and south of the river, Confederates realized that controlling the James from Richmond to below City Point would split the Union Army in two and cut off its waterborne supply. Yet their only attempt at securing what was a natural wedge between the two wings of the enemy and a plug to stop the flow of supplies failed because of poor seamanship and timid leadership.

FORT MONROE: 1861–1862

GEN. SIMON BERNARD, A FORMER aide-de-camp to Napoleon I and French expatriate, personally designed Fort Monroe on Old Point Comfort at the tip of the Virginia Peninsula. After Napoleon's defeat at Waterloo and subsequent exile to St. Helena, Bernard came to the United States. Arriving in Washington in 1816 with a letter of introduction from Lafayette himself, Bernard was made a brevet brigadier general in the U.S. Army and was put at the head of a board of engineers formed to construct the coastal defenses for the eastern United States.

Fort Monroe was often called "The Gibraltar of Chesapeake Bay," and indeed, even though it sat occupied by Federal troops in the heart of the Confederacy for four years of war, it was unassailable and provided the Union with a base for both overland and naval operations throughout the conflict. Its construction began in 1819 and continued until 1834, when it was completed for the most part by a youthful lieutenant of the U.S. Army Engineers named Robert E. Lee.

Fort Monroe was Lee's second assignment after being stationed at Cockspur Island, South Carolina, helping oversee the construction of Fort Pulaski. He reported for duty at Fort Monroe in May 1831. That June

> TO REACH FORT MONROE, TAKE Route I-64 heading southeast from the upper Virginia Peninsula. Follow 64 to Hampton, then exit to U.S. Route 258 and take that east then south, following signs to Fort Monroe and Old Point Comfort.

he married Mary Anne Randolph Custis, the daughter of George Washington's adopted son. The couple returned to Fort Monroe to spend the next three and a half years living on the post, though Mary Anne spent at least as much time back at Arlington as she did at Fort Monroe.[1] Their first son, future Confederate general George Washington Custis Lee, was born at the fort.

Since Lee's superior officer at the fort was called away often, the young lieutenant got a great deal of firsthand experience in the design and building of major fortifications. Lee supervised the excavation of the moat, completion of the stone scarp and counterscarp (the walls that contain the moat) and the Water Battery (which no longer exists), and began working on Fort Wool, situated on a man-made island called the "Rip-raps" in the middle of the channel off Old Point Comfort. While he gained valuable

The moat, scarp, and counter-scarp (the walls that contain the moat) constructed by Robert E. Lee while at Fort Monroe in 1834.

experience in the economics of construction projects and in handling men, perhaps the most vital lesson he learned was the importance of well-designed fortified works in defending a position from assault.

From the beginning of the Civil War, whenever Lee's men halted in the presence of the enemy, they were made to dig in and set up makeshift field fortifications. Though not as elaborate as the intricately designed walls, parapets, and casemates that provided interlocking fields of fire at Fort Monroe, Lee's field fortifications and earthworks were based on many of the same principles. Lee's men

ridiculed him early in the war, feeling they should stand out in the open and fight like "real soldiers" instead of digging in with picks and shovels, and they called him "The King of Spades." But those whose lives were saved when minié balls bit into the log breastwork instead of their bodies had no further desire to call their general names.

While working at Fort Monroe, Lee also had an opportunity to become acquainted with numerous officers who attended an artillery school there. Among his acquaintances were James Barnes, Benjamin Huger, and Joseph E. Johnston. Barnes would become a general in the Union Army, and Huger and Johnston generals in the Confederate Army alongside Lee.

After several months of construction work on Fort Wool, Lee accepted a position in the chief engineer's office in Washington. He left Fort Monroe and reported for duty in Washington in November 1834.[2]

In April 1861, when the Civil War broke out, military planners in the North realized just how strategically important Fort Monroe was. From its location at the mouth of the James, artillery within the fort and naval forces based there could control warship and supply-ship traffic up the James, Nansemond, Elizabeth, Chickahominy, and Appomattox rivers. If the Federal forces could maintain control of Fort Monroe and seal off those rivers, they would also control the flow of supplies in and out of the important Southern ports of Norfolk, Suffolk, Portsmouth, Richmond, and Petersburg. In addition, Fort Monroe could be used as a staging and supply area for landborne operations less than eighty-five miles from the enemy capital, Richmond, and as a fueling and supply base for seaborne operations far closer to the enemy than the nearest Northern port. That's why on April 14, 1861—the day after Fort Sumter fell—U.S. forces were rushed to Fort Monroe by sea, and, within a month and a half, the fort's normal garrison of 400 grew to nearly 6,000 troops, most of which had to be distributed to adjacent areas supporting the fort.[3]

On April 20, 1861, Union troops were transported to the Gosport Navy Yard near Norfolk in order to set fire to it to deny the Confederates its shipbuilding potential. One ship they didn't burn completely would come

---

☛ **W H A T · T O · S E E** The Casemate Museum is housed within the thick walls of Fort Monroe and is a must to see. Exhibits of artillery emplacements within the fort, living quarters and conditions, and the cell in which the president of the Confederacy, Jefferson Davis, was incarcerated after his capture are interpreted. From the outside parapet, Hampton Roads spreads out below. The site of the battle between the *Monitor* and the *Merrimack* can be seen from the point of view of the officers and men of the fort, who watched the event on March 9, 1862. The picturesque Old Point Comfort Lighthouse still stands outside the fort, and from the riverside park, nuclear-powered guided missile cruisers, aircraft carriers, and submarines can be seen plying the waters where their sail- and coal-powered predecessors once roamed and fought.

back to haunt them. The steam frigate *Merrimack* burned only to the waterline and was raised by the Confederates when they occupied Norfolk. It was refitted with a sloping casemate and iron plating. The result was the Confederate ironclad *Virginia*, and less than a year later she would be steaming through Hampton Roads again.

On May 27, 1861, Gen. Benjamin Butler sent Federal troops to occupy Newport News, isolating Norfolk even further from Confederate forces upriver, and though Union forces were driven back from their advance to Big Bethel on June 10 and Confederates virtually surrounded them at Fort Monroe from above on the peninsula and across Hampton Roads, control of the James was firmly in Union hands. ▪

HAMPTON ROADS: The Battle of the Ironclads

THE SPECTACLE WAS NOT ONLY REmarkable but history making. On March 8, 1862, black smoke billowing from its stack, the resurrected *Merrimack,* rechristened the *Virginia* by Confederates, ponderously made her way down the Elizabeth River from Norfolk and steamed slowly into Hampton Roads, the common waterway where the James, Nansemond, and Elizabeth rivers mix before flowing past Fort Monroe into the Chesapeake. Methodically she began destroying the Union fleet stationed to protect the Federal forts around Hampton Roads. The *Virginia* (just as often called the *Merrimack* by Federals and Confederates alike) headed right for the USS *Cumberland* and rammed her, then damaged the *Congress* and the *Minnesota* and drove them aground. The garrison of Fort Monroe watched,

HAMPTON ROADS CAN BE SEEN from the parapet of Fort Monroe as well as from the Monitor-Merrimack overlook at the site of Camp Butler in Newport News.

horrified, from the parapets as the cannons on the *Cumberland* continued firing until she sank below the waves. They knew that gunners were still manning their battle stations or were trapped below decks by heavy shifting guns and implements, tangled lines, and closed hatches and were drowning before their eyes as the ship settled slowly in the mud of Hampton Roads.

A Confederate eyewitness, watching from Ragged Island about three and one-half miles away, described the *Virginia's* rampage like this:

She passed on up, exchanging broadsides with the Congress, and making straight for the Cumberland, at which she made a dash, firing her bow-guns as she struck the doomed vessel with her prow. I could hardly believe my senses when I saw the masts of the Cumberland begin to sway wildly. After one or two lurches, her hull disappeared beneath the water, guns firing to the last moment. Most of her brave crew went down with their ship, but not with their colors, for the Union flag still floated defiantly from the masts, which projected obliquely for about half their length above the water after the vessel had settled unevenly upon the river bottom. This first act of the drama was over in about thirty minutes, but it seemed to me only a moment.[4]

A ship of the *Virginia's* like had never been seen before in American waters. Beginning with the hull of the old *Merrimack*, Confederate naval engineers constructed seven-foot-high walls of pitch pine and oak twenty-two inches thick sloping between thirty-five and forty-five degrees, then covered them with four inches of iron plating, rolled at the Tredegar Iron Works in Richmond. The heaviest shot from U.S. naval guns merely bounced off her sides, and her own rifled cannons blasted holes through the heavy wooden planking of the Union vessels. To her prow, they fastened a cast-iron, wedge-shaped ram, which broke in the collision with the *Cumberland*. The *Virginia* drew twenty-one feet of water forward and twenty-two feet aft. But because of her extreme weight and the fact that the old *Merrimack's* engines had been condemned and never replaced during the conversion to ironclad, she could not travel through the water faster than a mere five miles per hour. She was armed with two seven-inch rifles, two six-inch rifles, and six nine-inch smoothbores totalling ten guns.[5]

She was not the first ironclad. They had been used in other parts of the world before—against the Russians by the French, and by the British, whose *Warrior* was built of iron, not just covered by it. By the time the *Virginia* sent the sailors on the *Cumberland* to their muddy graves, close to a hundred iron-armored ships were on the seas or in the docks being built in Europe.

In America too there had already been ironclads at least on the drawing board. At the end of the War of 1812, a slope-sided, steam-powered, iron-plated ship was under construction. For twenty years, beginning in 1842, two New Jersey brothers named Stevens worked under Congressional appropriations to construct a ram sheathed in iron, but after delays, design changes to accommodate technological advances in artillery, and lengthy litigation, the U.S. government lost interest.

By 1862 there was another ironclad to consider.[6] Though cumbersome and

The Battle of the Ironclads at Hampton Roads

unwieldy, by the time she slowly retired from Hampton Roads leaving the wooden ships burning behind her, the *Virginia* had made a statement that reverberated from Hampton Roads to every sea that carries fighting ships to this day: The four-thousand-year era of wooden fighting ships had ended, and the era of floating and fighting iron and steel had unequivocally begun.

The next day the *Virginia* returned to finish off the *Minnesota* and the other wooden ships left guarding the forts. Her mission was simple enough: Destroy the Union naval forces supporting Fort Monroe, Fort Wool, and Camp Butler in Newport News, then prevent any other ships from entering the waterway. Without the Yankee gunships, the forts, surrounded by Confederate land forces, would be cut off from food and supplies. With the fall of Fort Monroe, the James, Nansemond, Elizabeth, Chickahominy, and Appomattox rivers would be securely in Confederate hands, and Norfolk, Suffolk, Portsmouth, Richmond, and Petersburg would be safe from waterborne or river-supported invasions.

At 8:45 A.M. on March 9, 1862, that objective seemed entirely within the grasp of the *Virginia* and her crew. By 9:00 A.M., however, that view was radically changed. Having heard rumors months before of the building of a Confederate ironclad warship, Northern planners had begun designing and building one of their own. On the night of March 9, by the flickering light of the burning *Congress*, the USS *Monitor* anchored protectively beside the *Minnesota*.

The Confederate *Virginia's* design relied upon thick, sloped iron plating to make her impervious to enemy shells. The Union's ironclad vessel was designed with a low profile to make her a small, hard-to-hit target. She was one hundred seventy-two feet long with a forty-one-foot beam, but her waterline profile, excluding the turret and pilothouse, was only one and one-half feet. She needed only ten feet of water beneath her keel to operate. Inside her single revolving turret, the *Monitor* carried two huge eleven-inch cannons each firing a shot weighing one hundred eighty pounds.

For over three hours the antagonists

maneuvered about, rammed, and blasted one another in Hampton Roads. Officers and men from Fort Monroe again lined the parapets to watch, hardly able to see the tiny *Monitor* with its barely visible turret riding a little more than twelve feet above the surface of Hampton Roads, and knowing what would happen to them if the ship went down.

The smaller *Monitor*, with her shallow draft, maneuvered better. White marks had been painted on the deck inside the turret to indicate fore and aft, starboard and port, but the black powder and scuffing of gunners' feet soon caused them to disappear, so the executive officer commanding the gun-crew of the *Monitor* had to constantly call out to ask bearings on the

Virginia. The *Monitor's* two guns could fire only once every eight minutes, but the Union ship's high maneuverability made the *Virginia* miss a ramming attempt.

No doubt the hearts of many watching from Fort Monroe sank as the *Monitor* disengaged and began to draw away from the combat. The *Monitor* was withdrawing only temporarily, however, to attend to Lt. John L. Worden, the ship's commander, who had been wounded in the face. When the *Monitor* returned to the scene of action, the *Virginia* also had withdrawn to attend to her wounded and damages.

Later, Confederates would count some ninety-eight impressions in the armor of the *Virginia*, estimating that

☛ **W H A T · T O · S E E** A map near the flagstaff on the parapet of Fort Monroe shows where the two ironclads fought, but trees obscure some of the view in the summer. After viewing the map for orientation, it is best to exit the fort and park in the lot across the street. Walking to Old Point Comfort, or just to the edge of the water, will give you a good view of the area of Hampton Roads where the two ships maneuvered and blasted each other for three hours, as well as a view of the site of the *Merrimack's* victories over the Union fleet the day before the battle.

about twenty came from the engagement with the *Monitor*. Photographs taken of the *Monitor* show deep indentations on the turret from the *Virginia's* cannon.

The importance of the battle between these two ships cannot be underestimated, both in terms of the worldwide impact upon the design of fighting ships and especially in the advantages given the Union by the *Virginia's* failure to drive away the *Monitor*.

Historians have called the battle a draw. Tactically it was. But strategically the Federals were the winners, because the Confederates needed desperately to gain control of the James River. As long as the *Monitor* remained afloat in Hampton Roads, the Confederates could not use the great river to supply their armies in Virginia from their seaports further south. And even worse, they could not deny its use to the Federals as long as the *Monitor* held the *Virginia* in stalemate. Denying the Federals the James and its numerous upriver ports with railroads leading from them would have radically altered Union strategy for the rest of the war. As it turned out, however, the *Virginia's* role in threatening the Union hold on the James River and the impact her presence in the James had on Union operations was not over yet. ▪

NORFOLK

AFTER NEARLY 100 YEARS AS A bustling Colonial seaport, Norfolk's waterfront was shelled on January 1, 1776, by British ships under the command of Lord Dunmore. What wasn't destroyed by the British bombardment was put to the torch by townsfolk to deny it to the enemy. Yet the advantageous location where the James, York, Elizabeth, and Nansemond rivers converge and empty into the Chesapeake Bay dictated that Norfolk would be rebuilt. In 1855 Norfolk's importance as a seaport brought another shipborne disaster, this time in the form of an

TO REACH NORFOLK, FOLLOW I-64 down the Virginia Peninsula. From the south, follow Virginia Route 17 to I-64. From the west take U.S. Route 58 or U.S. Route 460 from Petersburg. To get to the Hampton Roads Naval Museum without taking an organized tour, take I-64 to Norfolk and exit onto 564. Take 564 to the Norfolk Naval Base and obtain a pass from the Tour and Information Center located at 9809 Hampton Boulevard.

epidemic of yellow fever. Estimates of the death toll range from one-tenth to one-third of the city's population. Norfolk barely had time to mourn its dead before the Civil War brought more devastation. In April 1861 United States forces abandoned Norfolk and attempted to burn everything of military use at the Gosport Navy Yard, just across the Elizabeth River in Portsmouth. Fortunately for the Union, Fort Monroe remained in Northern hands. This provided a base for future Federal operations in Virginia and the eventual retaking of Norfolk in May 1862 by direct order of President Lincoln.

Norfolk's importance after the Civil War continued to be tied to its location on the Chesapeake. In 1917 the U.S. Navy established an operations base and training center at Norfolk. During World War II, Norfolk's population doubled as military men and their families moved to the city, turning it into what has been called the largest military installation in the world. It retains that status to this day. ▪

☛ **W H A T · T O · S E E** Norfolk, Virginia, one of the larger, older, and still militarily important cities in the United States, has a great number of attractions to see and tours by which to see these sites. There are beautiful hotels, parks, and marketplaces, as well as the Norfolk Botanical Garden, the Virginia Zoological Park, an opera company, a symphony, and a professional theater troupe. Norfolk is also the home of the Chrysler Art Museum, which houses works collected by Walter P. Chrysler, Jr., including pieces by Degas, Manet, Cezanne, and Gauguin. For an information packet, write or call the Norfolk Convention and Visitors Bureau, 236 E. Plume Street, Norfolk, VA 23510, telephone (800) 368-3097.

One particularly appealing set of tours is the Trolley Tours offered by Tidewater Regional Transit (see "Trolley Tours of Norfolk" in *Appendix B*). Discounts are available on the various tours, trolleys, shuttles, and ferries needed to move between Norfolk and Virginia Beach. Available tours include Norfolk, the Norfolk Naval Base, Olde Towne Portsmouth, and Oceana Air Station. Tours run about every thirty minutes during the peak season (June 10 through September 2), five times a day in the spring and fall, and twice a day on weekends only over the winter months. Reservations are recommended during the off-season but are not needed during the

continued on page 88

continued from page 87
summer months. You can get off the trolley to see one of the sites along the tour, then catch the next trolley to continue the tour.

Along with some of the more modern attractions, the trolley takes you to the MacArthur Memorial, where the general is buried. The Memorial also houses documents from World War II, MacArthur's staff car, and eleven exhibit galleries immortalizing his life and military career.

The Hampton Roads Naval Museum at the Norfolk Naval Base includes Civil War exhibits. The museum is housed in the Pennsylvania Building, which is a two-thirds scale replica of Philadelphia's Independence Hall.

Gosport Navy Yard (the original site of which is across the Elizabeth River at Portsmouth), which supplied the early U.S. Navy with ships, is commemorated at the naval museum, and the story is told of the burning and abandonment of the shipyard by Union troops at the beginning of the Civil War. In fact, an entire wing of the museum is used to explain the important role of Hampton Roads in the Civil War.

Of particular interest to Civil War enthusiasts are the exhibits portraying the action between the *Monitor* and the *Virginia*. A fiber-optic map explains the battle in Hampton Roads in March 1862, and there is a full-scale reproduction of the turret of the *Monitor*. Artifacts include items recovered from the sinking of the *Monitor* (in a storm later in the war) and from the USS *Cumberland*, the first ship to be sunk by the Confederate ironclad *Virginia*.

The museum also houses a research library, available to scholars of naval history by appointment only.

Operated by the Hampton Roads Naval Historical Foundation, the museum is open from 9:00 A.M. to 4:00 P.M. seven days a week. Admission is free, and passes allowing you to visit the museum are available from the Tour and Information Office located outside Gate Two on Hampton Boulevard. For information call (804) 444-2243 or (804) 444-8971.

PORTSMOUTH

LAND ON THE ELIZABETH RIVER CON-fiscated from one of the earliest settlers who had participated in Bacon's Rebellion was eventually laid out into lots and streets by Col. William Crawford. By 1752 the town had a name reflecting its inseparable ties with the water: Portsmouth.

Nearby, the village of Gosport grew up around the shipbuilding industry, and by 1775 it was being used by the British Navy as a repair station. The Revolution and the War of 1812 brought more British—and more turmoil—to Portsmouth. By 1784 Gosport had become a part of

PORTSMOUTH CAN BE REACHED by following U.S. Route 58 or 460 from the west, or U.S. Route 17 from the south to I-64. I-64 leads to I-264, which bisects Portsmouth.

Portsmouth, and by 1801 the U.S. government purchased the Gosport Navy Yard.

Portsmouth suffered from the yellow fever epidemic in 1855 like her sister city Norfolk and lost nearly a quarter of her population. Portsmouth was abandoned by Federal troops when

☛ **W H A T · T O · S E E**   The best way to see Portsmouth, Virginia, may again be the trolley package, which includes a ferry ride from Norfolk to Portsmouth. Among some of the historic houses on the trolley tour are the Peters House on Court Street, which served as Union general Benjamin Butler's headquarters during his tenure in Portsmouth, and the Pass House, the Union adjutant general's headquarters during the city's occupation, where any civilian had to obtain a pass to leave Portsmouth.

The Portsmouth Lightship Museum is housed in an original 1915 U.S. Coast Guard lightship on Water Street and interprets the role of the lightship service, which began in 1820 off Craney Island (where the *Virginia* was scuttled in 1862).

The Portsmouth Naval Shipyard Museum stands at the foot of High Street and contains models, exhibits, and artifacts detailing the history of the navy in this area. Displays and relics emphasize in particular the role of the shipyard in the outfitting of the frigate *Merrimack*, and her transformation into the Confederate ironclad *Virginia*.

Virginia seceded in 1861, and the Navy Yard was burned by retreating Union soldiers. When Confederate troops were forced to evacuate the city in 1862, they also burned the Navy Yard. ∎

NEWPORT NEWS

LEGEND ATTRIBUTED THE NAME NEWport News to several sources: Port Newce in Ireland from where one of the earliest settlers hailed; the Newce brothers, who originally patented the land; and Capt. Christopher Newport, an early explorer of the area. The area remained mostly farmland until the railroad came, and a shipyard was established in the town. During the Civil War, Confederate general John Magruder established an elaborate system of defenses, consisting of earthworks, dams, and levees with the ability to flood low-lying areas in case of Federal attacks. ∎

NEWPORT NEWS IS REACHED by following I-64 or Virginia State Route 60 southeast down the Virginia Peninsula. The War Memorial Museum of Virginia is located on U.S. Route 60 adjacent the James River Bridge. From I-64 take the Mercury Boulevard/James River Bridge exit south; follow Mercury Boulevard (U.S. 258) to Warwick Boulevard (U.S. 60). The museum is located at 9285 Warwick Boulevard in Newport News. To reach the Mariner's Museum, take exit 62-A off I-64 to Museum Drive in Newport News; to reach the park, take exit 250-B off I-64.

☛ **W H A T · T O · S E E** Military history buffs will enjoy the War Memorial Museum of Virginia, which houses exhibits on the evolution of weaponry, women at war, the black soldier, the Axis powers, and America and war. The museum contains more than sixty thousand artifacts, including weapons, uniforms, flags, artillery, vehicles, propaganda posters, photographs, and insignia. Many of these artifacts are Civil War-related. There is also a research library with letters, maps, rare books, manuals, photos, and newspapers; it is open by appointment only.

continued on page 91

continued from page 90

The Mariner's Museum interprets the maritime history of a part of America linked with the sea. The museum holds a collection of small craft from around the world, handmade scale models, mariner's art such as scrimshaw and figureheads, and exhibits containing working models of classic steam engines and historic recreational boats by Chris-Craft. Special exhibits are in the Great Hall of Steam and the Chesapeake Bay Gallery. A research library houses 67,000 volumes and more than 350,000 photographs.

Newport News Park, one of the largest municipal parks in the country, contains 8,500 acres and a 189-site campground. Boats are available for use on the reservoir, and nearly eleven miles of the original earthworks laid out by General Magruder can still be seen. Rangers lead tours around the site from park headquarters.

THE PENINSULA CAMPAIGN: March to May 1862

THE SPECTER OF THE IRONCLAD VIR-*ginia*, sailing out in the vicinity of Fort Monroe in the spring of 1862, affected the military strategists of the North immensely. The year before, Northern strategists had attempted the overland route to Richmond and were turned back at the Battle of Manassas, July 21, 1861. Now, Union general George B. McClellan, the great organizer, after abandoning his plan to use Urbanna on the Rappahannock River as his base of supplies for an overland march on Richmond, chose to use Fort Monroe as his base. McClellan was prepared to embark his forces at Alexandria, Virginia, on the Potomac,

WHILE ROUTE 5 IS THE REC-ommended way to see the many sites associated with the James River, visitors to this area of Virginia should not pass up a tour of the battlefields from McClellan's 1862 Peninsula Campaign. The best place to start is the National Park Service's Chimborazo Visitor Center, 3215 East Broad St., Richmond. The Park Service's tour takes you through the battlefields of Beaver Dam Creek, Cold Harbor (both 1862 and 1864 battles), Gaines's Mill, Savage Station (with *continued on page 92*

when news of the *Virginia's* successes in Hampton Roads brought his plans to a halt. How could he load hundreds of wooden ships with men and supplies and send them into the waterways controlled by such a dangerous vessel as the *Virginia?* In an afternoon, that one ship could sink a dozen or more transports, sending tons of supplies and thousands of men to the mud of Hampton Roads. It wasn't until he was assured that the *Virginia* was in drydock undergoing repairs from her battle with the *Monitor* that McClellan launched his amphibious campaign against the Confederates on the Peninsula.[7]

Beginning on March 17, 1862, more than 120,000 men were transported on nearly four hundred ships of various types from the dock at Alexandria, Virginia, down the Potomac to Fort Monroe and landed there before moving up the broad peninsula of land lying between the York and James rivers. With thousands of head of cattle, anywhere from 1,150 to 3,500 wagons, 700 ambulances, nearly 270 artillery pieces including caissons, and 15,000 horses and mules, it would stand as the largest amphibious movement undertaken by a U.S. commander until June 1944 when Gen. Dwight D. Eisenhower commanded the Allied forces in the invasion of France on D-Day.[8]

Utilizing first the Potomac then the York for both transportation and sup-

continued from page 91
a side trip to Fair Oaks and Seven Pines), White Oak Swamp, Glendale, and Malvern Hill before the tour route intersects Route 5. A right turn on Route 5 will take you toward Fort Harrison and Fort Brady; a left turn on Routes 5/156 will take you to the James River Plantations along Route 5, or across the James (on Route 156 then right on Route 10) to City Point, Bermuda Hundred, and Drewry's Bluff.

plies was a logistical marvel brought off by General McClellan and his staff. By the first day of April 1862, McClellan's forces had safely disembarked at Fort Monroe and Newport News. In planning his campaign up the peninsula, McClellan had hoped that the Union Navy would be able not only to guard his supply routes along the York and James rivers but also to lend additional artillery support from the rivers. The *Virginia*, still lurking in the James, would threaten any Union gunboat on that river—including the *Monitor*—that tried to support McClellan's advance.

With the *Monitor* keeping the *Virginia* at bay in the James, however, McClellan would have the navy's support from the York River, so his first objectives would have to lie near that body of water. West Point, where the

York River was fed by the Mattaponi and Pamunkey rivers, was the spot from which the railroad could supply his army in its advance upon Richmond. To take West Point, McClellan would have to open the York, which was being defended by the Confederates with artillery batteries at Gloucester Point and the old Revolutionary War battle site of Yorktown.

Flag Officer Louis M. Goldsborough, commanding the Union flotilla at Hampton Roads, because of the nagging presence of the *Virginia* and his desire to keep the ironclad from roaming the rivers (including the Potomac) that empty into the Chesapeake, could not send his powerful warships from the James River to bombard the Confederate batteries on the York. So McClellan was locked into executing a time-consuming siege operation to drive the Confederates from Yorktown. (See *The York River* chapter for details on operations around Yorktown.)

Then Abraham Lincoln visited Fort Monroe and, seeing the inaction caused by the *Virginia's* presence, ordered Union troops to take Norfolk, base for the ironclad, on May 9, 1862. Federals made an amphibious landing at Ocean View and advanced overland to accept the surrender of the city of Norfolk by its mayor. By then the Gosport Navy Yard was in flames, fired by retreating Confederates. Confederates were unable to sail the *Virginia* upriver to Richmond: Her draft, now increased to twenty-three feet because

☛ **W H A T · T O · S E E** Numerous roadside exhibits and signs explain the battles fought by Joseph Johnston, and later, Robert E. Lee, that drove the Union Army under McClellan back down the peninsula and forced him to change his base from White House on the Pamunkey to Harrison's Landing on the James. Each of the Seven Days' Battles is interpreted and Cold Harbor has an exhibit shelter explaining the fighting in both 1862 and 1864. The Watt House (closed to the public) on the Gaines's Mill battlefield has been restored, and there is a walking trail to where Confederate troops from Texas and Georgia broke through Union lines. Remnants of Union trenches can still be seen. The Garthright House (closed to the public), with some sections dating to the early eighteenth century, was used as a hospital during the Battle of Cold Harbor. The National Cemetery near the battlefield of Glendale contains the remains of Union soldiers who fell during the fighting in this area, and exhibits at Malvern Hill explain the horrible devastation wrought by Union cannons lined up hub-to-hub, firing against packed Confederate infantry.

of repairs and refinements, made it impossible for her to negotiate the river upstream. Off Craney Island, at 5:00 A.M. on May 11, she was blown up and scuttled. McClellan and the Union flotilla were now finally able to use the James River as they saw fit.

The importance of the loss of the *Virginia* to the Confederates cannot be overestimated. Her removal from the James—and her removal in the minds of Federal strategists—was one of the major factors affecting the Union campaigns into Virginia in both 1862 and 1864. ▪

DREWRY'S BLUFF

UPON MCCLELLAN'S URGING AFTER hearing of the scuttling of the *Virginia*, five Union gunboats, including the *Monitor* and the *Galena*, started up the James. By May 15, 1862, they were only seven miles below Richmond and ready to round a big bend in the James and pass a ninety-foot cliff on the south bank of the river.

In mid-March of 1862, when Confederate forces at Yorktown were first being threatened by McClellan's advance up the Peninsula, Capt. Augustus Drewry had begun constructing a fort on the bluff that bears his name. On May 13, 1862, Drewry and his troops heard from a steamer coming upriver that the Yankee gunboats were on their way. With two days' warning, more artillery was brought to the fort, sharpshooters and riflemen dug in on the banks of the James, and the famed Washington Artillery from New Orleans entrenched themselves on the opposite bank of the river, providing

TO REACH DREWRY'S BLUFF, follow the National Park Service signs off of U.S. Route 1 south of the James River to the parking lot. A short walk will take you to the overlook on the James.

converging artillery fire across the waterway.

Overnight, in pouring rain, more Confederate troops under Gen. William Mahone arrived to dig rifle pits, fill sandbags, and take up positions supporting the artillery. Early the next morning, the Union flotilla steamed around the bend, heading toward Richmond.

The battle of Drewry's Bluff lasted nearly three and a half hours. Fire from the Confederate batteries dropped in on the Federal gunboats, and the heavy guns of the Union flotilla attempted to knock out the Confederate artillery so they could pass the

A fierce battle between Confederate artillery and Union gunboats took place at Drewry's Bluff on the James River on May 15, 1862.

bluffs. Some historians believe that if the flotilla had been supported by an infantry assault behind Drewry's Bluff, the Confederates would have had to evacuate Richmond. As it was, the Union gunboats retreated back down the river, and the idea of a naval offensive against the Confederate capital was abandoned. ▪

☛ **WHAT · TO · SEE** From inside restored Fort Darling, Drewry's Bluff affords a remarkable view of the James River, once again illustrating why hills overlooking rivers were militarily important. Even in the summer, with foliage abundant, some spires in Richmond can be seen several miles upstream, and the view is unobstructed downstream to the first bend in the river. This downstream section of the river is the battle site of May 15, 1862, where Union gunboats engaged the batteries within Fort Darling perched on Drewry's Bluff. Just below the fort and slightly upstream is where Civil War-period illustrations place the boats sunk as obstructions to the Union Navy's ascent of the James. The fort has been preserved and partially restored, and important sites within, such as the well, a powder magazine, and a gun emplacement, have been marked along the short, self-guided walking tour.

JAMES RIVER PLANTATIONS

THE GREAT PLANTATIONS along the James, started in the 1600s, brought much wealth and fame to their owners. These plantations have had such an effect upon the imagination of Americans that many of them remain today as reminders of a glorious, fabled, bittersweet way of life that, in a way, both brought on the Civil War and was consumed by it.

Most of recorded American history can be traced along the social and economic tendrils of a weed. From the very beginning, tobacco—grown originally by the Native Americans and passed on to the European transplants, then shipped to England and the Continent—gave all who tried it a pleasurable, habit-forming pastime. The demand for tobacco from the Virginia colonies would increase until it became the main cash crop of most of the plantations along the James.

Just look at what tobacco money has done (and continues to do) in Virginia. For the early landowners along the James, tobacco, shipped in huge hogshead barrels from docks located at the riverside, brought in immense profits and assured the longevity of slavery. Though only about seven percent of the population in the South owned slaves, it was the wealthy who were the slaveholders and, with their political power, exercised the "rights" of the slaveowners far beyond their legitimate leverage. Names linked to the plantations, like Carter, Byrd, Harrison, and Jefferson, resound still in Virginia—and American—history.

Though the crop was very hard on the land, the money from tobacco bought the materials for expensive homes and then provided the means to expand them. The more recent love for history and tradition by Tidewater Virginians, some of whom are descendants of the original owners, has encouraged restoration of the magnificent mansions and brought visitors to places with romantic names like Shirley, Berkeley, Westover, Evelynton, and Sherwood Forest. But in the tumultuous 1860s, the war brought other visitors to them: the armies and their thousands of men, wounded and helpless from battle, sick and dying from disease, or healthy and ready to forage—or pillage—whatever they could.

THE PENINSULA CAMPAIGN:
June to August 1862

IN SPITE OF THE SUPPORT OF THE UNION Navy on both the James and York rivers after the destruction of the *Virginia*, Gen. George McClellan was caught in the awkward position of having half his Federal army on one side of the Chickahominy and the other half on the other side when the Confederates attacked. From June 25, 1862, to July 1, 1862, Gen. Robert E. Lee, in a whirlwind week of running fights known as the Seven Days' Battles, drove McClellan from the very suburbs of Richmond across the Chickahominy River to the south side of the peninsula and the James. McClellan, in another incredible feat of logistics—and an even greater feat of obfuscation—managed to withdraw half his army in a massive retreat before Lee's forces and move his base of supplies southward from White House on the Pamunkey River completely across the peninsula to Harrison's Landing on the James, calling it merely a "change of base."

Listening to everyone for information on the enemy from the moment he engaged in battle, from a fugitive slave to his own frail confidence, McClellan was a whipped man almost from the start and began withdrawing his army accordingly. As early as the evening of June 25, just after his first battle at Oak Grove (also known as Seven Pines), he began preparing for the evacuation of his base at White House on the Pamunkey River. By July 1, Robert E. Lee and his Army of Northern Virginia, though feeling that they had not fought well, were in complete mastery of both McClellan's mind and his army in the field. The Union general had issued his final orders for retreat even before he had heard of his army's victory at Malvern Hill.[9]

The place to which McClellan chose to retreat was known as Harrison's Landing, on two lovely plantations on the James River called Berkeley and Westover.

For directions to and what to see on the Peninsula, see "The Peninsula Campaign: March to May 1862." ▪

HARRISON'S LANDING

THE AREA THAT WAS TO BECOME Berkeley Plantation was first settled by the English in 1619. By 1726 the Harrison family had acquired it and built the large, brick dwelling house. Among the Harrisons who were born and lived on the plantation were Benjamin Harrison V, a signer of the Declaration of Independence, and President William Henry Harrison. The century and a quarter of Harrison ownership left its legacy in the name of the landings on the James, and it was to Harrison's Landing that the Union Army retreated after Malvern Hill.

Under a pouring rain, McClellan's Union Army, demoralized and feeling defeated even after their victory at Malvern Hill, trampled the fields of grain and wheat as they passed the mansion house at Berkeley on July 2–3, 1862, and moved onto the broad plain that led to the ships on the James.

Though under the cover of the guns of the Union Navy and with transports in the river just a few yards away, McClellan still felt edgy. Matters were not helped when the Confederate cavalry leader Jeb Stuart discovered that a long ridge called Evelynton Heights (sometimes referred to as "Evelington") on the plantation of Evelynton overlooked the Union

THE PLANTATIONS OF SHIRLEY, Berkeley, Westover, and Evelynton are all accessible from Route 5. The signs for the individual plantations are unobtrusive, so watch for them carefully. For those of you cruising this section of the James with your own boats, Westover can be identified by a private dock with a boat lift (not open to the public). Recent charts show the buoy in the channel nearest to Westover to be marked RN "96" (red nun buoy #96). Some pilings are visible just downstream from the modern private dock. They appear to be in the same location as the U.S. mailboat wharf shown in drawings. They are driven into the riverbed where a sunken road cuts down to the riverbank, just on the downstream side of a wall marking the end of the lawn at Westover.

Shallow draft fishing skiffs were seen making their way up Herring Creek below Evelynton. There is a dock on Herring Creek at Evelynton, but personnel at the plantation say that if you wish to arrive by private boat, you should call first and ask permission to tie continued on page 99

camp where it sat between the James River and Herring Creek. At 9:00 A.M. Stuart's brilliant horse artillery officer, Capt. John Pelham, let loose with the one howitzer he had brought for this foray, dropping shells and firing some unpredictable Congreve rockets from the Heights into the soggy Union soldiers.

For five hours the bombardment went on, with Union infantry and artillery making its way toward Evelynton Heights to dislodge the pesky Confederates and Jeb Stuart wondering where his own infantry under Stonewall Jackson and James Longstreet was. On the winding backroads north of that stretch of the river, the Southern commanders had gotten lost with their troops and didn't get to Evelynton until after dark. The story might have had a different ending if they had arrived with all their artillery to bombard the Yankees' camp from the long ridge overlooking Harrison's Landing.

The plantation of Berkeley became a hospital for the wounded during the latter days of the campaign. Something like four thousand wagons, all coming from the abandoned base at White House, converged upon the plantation and Harrison's Landing.

After Pelham shelled the Union position and Stuart was driven from Evelynton Heights, McClellan went to work fortifying the high ground above

continued from page 98

up and take the tour of the plantation. It will take a shallow draft boat, because the entrance to Herring Creek is only four feet deep, and a person on the bow to watch for stakes and snags. The creek itself is eight to twelve feet deep. The entrance to Herring Creek from the James appears to be about 330 degrees magnetic bearing from channel buoy R "92." It also appears to be in range with channel buoy R "92" and G "91" on the other side of the channel. Once again, be careful approaching the entrance. (Caution: These instructions are not intended for navigational purposes. Always consult a current National Oceanic Service chart, Local Notices to Mariners, or, in the case of small creeks like Herring Creek, local fishermen and boaters.)

Harrison's Landing from Kimage's Creek on the left flank to Herring's Creek on his right. Northern gunboats supported him from the James, as Union signalmen established wig-wag stations atop both Berkeley and Westover mansions. McClellan set up his own headquarters at Berkeley. Almost daily, observation balloons lifted off from the yard at Berkeley and even from a ship in the James—the first

U.S. aircraft carrier—for reconnaissance purposes. By July 8, the area was safe enough for Abraham Lincoln to visit and review the army.

Harrison's Landing soon became as active as a large seaport city. An estimated six hundred ships of all types moved from Harrison's Landing to Newport News, and six wharves were temporary ports for a hundred ships at any one time.[10]

Once the *Virginia* was no longer a factor, Harrison's Landing was an excellent base for offensive operations. McClellan chose, however, to postpone launching another drive up the peninsula or a crossing of the James for a movement on Richmond from the south until the end of the summer, when events in other theaters of the war forced Lincoln to recall his army.

McClellan's army, inactive at Harrison's Landing, soon became nothing more than a bored, fly- and louse-infested, suffering, sick, although well-trained, mob. Daily drills did nothing to help the morale of the troops, who saw hundreds of their comrades dying from disease and thousands more carried off by boat to hospitals in Washington. Flies, attracted by the unsanitary conditions of open latrines and unburied remains of animals slaughtered for food, reproduced into an omnipresent, biting, disease-carrying plague. Though the men built "shebangs"—lean-tos made

out of scrap wood, tin, or even leafy branches—the heat in Virginia that summer was overwhelming.

But perhaps the worst thing the men had to endure was the inaction. For the entire month of July and the first two weeks of August 1862, the men drilled and trained and responded to rumors of Confederate activity, but they gradually became aware that their commander was not going to advance upon the enemy. Desertions grew, often in the form of men just overstaying their leaves home. Monotony became the ever-present enemy, and morale plummeted. One positive result of the boredom was that Union general Daniel Butterfield, at his headquarters at Berkeley, used the idle time to rearrange an existing bugle call into a short, mournful melody to signify to the army that it was time to lay down their arms and rest on the field of battle. He called it "Taps."

At the beginning of August there was a flurry of activity in the camps. Instead of signaling an advance against the enemy, however, it was a response to the Union high command's orders to begin preparing to march to Fort Monroe. McClellan had delayed too long.

Even Lee could not wait for McClellan to march toward Richmond. Another Union army was threatening from the north, and in mid-July Lee began sending units of his army defend-

☞ **W H A T · T O · S E E** Shirley Plantation, founded in 1613, has been restored as an 800-acre working plantation and is operated by the ninth and tenth generations of Hills and Carters, descendants of the original owners of the land. Shirley is the birthplace of Robert E. Lee's mother, Anne Hill Carter, and Lee himself received some of his primary education in the converted laundry house. Completed in 1738, the mansion house is, for the most part, in its original state. It is recognized widely as an American architectural treasure. Its famous elegant, carved walnut staircase ascends three floors without columns or any other visible means of structural support and is the only stairway of its kind in America. The house contains family portraits, furnishings, silver, original paneling, and carved woodwork unsurpassed in other colonial homes. The admission fee allows you to tour the house and grounds. It includes the laundry house, barns, stable, smoke-house, ice house (where ice was cut and hauled from the James in the winter and packed in sawdust to last most of the summer), and a two-story outdoor kitchen. Shirley is open 9:00 A.M. to 5:00 P.M. daily except Christmas, and special rates are available for children, military personnel, groups of more than 10 people, and seniors over 60 years of age.

Berkeley offers tours of the house and grounds where the Harrisons entertained ten presidents, including Washington and Jefferson. Thomas Jefferson had a hand in directing the installation of some of the woodwork and double arches in the "great rooms" of the mansion house. Ten acres of terraced formal boxwood gardens wait to be explored. From the rear of the house, near the overflow parking area, you can see the view of the James and the site of the 1862 Civil War camps. The Coach House Tavern, offering refreshments and traditional colonial dining, is on the premises. Group reservations are suggested. A fee is charged for the tour.

Westover offers a self-guided tour of the privately owned grounds. (The interior of the house is not included in the tour.) You are invited to walk across the lawn and observe the magnificent house and its unique doorway, which continues to be recognized as the "Westover Doorway." The house is an excellent example of classical Georgian architecture in America. Originally the two wings were identical and not connected to the main center dwelling. The east wing, which once contained the 4,000-volume library of William Byrd, owner of the plantation, was burned during the Civil War.

continued on page 102

continued from page 101

The present east wing was built in 1900, when both wings were connected to the main house. On the tour you will see the ice house and a well house that contains a dry well and passageways leading from beneath the house to the river to facilitate escape from Indian attack, as legend has it. The remnants of the Civil War road that led down to the U.S. Mail Boat Wharf appear to be located toward the river on the outside of the brick wall to the east of the property. North of the house are formal gardens and the tomb of William Byrd II. The grounds and gardens are open from 9:00 A.M. to 6:00 P.M. daily, and a fee is collected on the honor system. (For those interested in natural history, keep your eyes open for the young bald eagle spotted fishing in the James River near Westover in August 1992.)

Evelynton Plantation is open to the public, and although the original house and outbuildings were burned during the Civil War, they were restored by architect W. Duncan Lee, who also did the restoration of Carter's Grove Plantation, associated with Historic Williamsburg. Tours of the house and grounds are available daily from 9:00 A.M. to 5:00 P.M. The 2,500-acre farm is still operated and owned by descendants of Edmund Ruffin, the man whose contributions to agriculture, which included scientific testing of soil and publication of *The Farmer's Register,* led to a revitalization of the agriculture industry in Virginia in the nineteenth century. To Civil War soldiers, however, Ruffin was remembered as the man who fired the first shot of the Civil War at Fort Sumter, South Carolina, which perhaps explains the rough treatment of the house when Union troops encamped there. A small plaque and cannon mark one end of Evelynton Heights where Jeb Stuart and John Pelham shelled the Union Army on Herring Creek below. The James River can be seen in the distance.

ing Richmond to halt the new threat. Getting to know his opponent well, Lee must have been pleased that his boldness in sending much of his army northward on August 13 was not exploited. McClellan began retreating from Harrison's Landing on August 15.

Harrison's Landing and the magnificent mansions of Berkeley and Westover were never the same after the Army of the Potomac left. The docks were burned, and the multitude of ships' masts that once resembled a forest disappeared. The vast sea of tents vanished, and the owners of the mansions were left with the damage wrought by uncaring soldiers in a hostile land: crops destroyed for that year's growing season; livestock taken or killed for food; lovely lawns dug up for latrines; the walled-in family cemetery at Berkeley desecrated by its use as a corral; slaves gone with their liberators; and the mansion houses filled with mud, damaged, accidentally burned, and stripped of anything useful to officers and enlisted men trying to make themselves comfortable.

Within three months of the army's leaving, both Westover and Berkeley were sold by their owners.

The war was not finished with the area yet, however. In 1864 Ulysses Grant would bring another Union Army onto the peninsula between the York and the James and would use the great river James as a fast-flowing source of supplies for the last campaign of the war. McClellan's overcautious reticence in 1862 was made up for by Grant's inexorable aggressiveness in 1864. ▪

TRAVELING THE JAMES

IN TOURING BY automobile the Civil War–associated areas that were influenced by the proximity of the James River, the two main highways that lead to most of the sites are Virginia state Route 5 along the north side of the James and Virginia state Route 10 along the south side. Both roads travel within a mile or two of the river, and the riverside sites are close by.

Current Route 5 was once the main road leading to the back doors of many of the most elegant plantation houses along the James River. (The front doors of plantation houses normally were on the river side, because prior to improved roads, the main approach to the luxurious main dwelling houses was from the river.) The old road that is now Route 5 left Richmond and led to New Market. It then passed a rise called Malvern Hill, soon to be drenched in Southern blood on a July afternoon in 1862. A knowledgeable nineteenth-century local would have been familiar with the maze of roads across the big bend in the river between Malvern and Westover Plantation and eventually would be able to lead you to Charles City Court House. The road then made its dusty way through the beautiful loblolly pine forests native to the peninsula, crossed the Chickahominy River at Barrett's Ferry, then stretched on to the old colonial capital of Williamsburg. Route 5 today is still a two-lane highway with a speed limit of 55. The berm is almost nonexistent, so bicycling Route 5 is not recommended, although more adventurous cyclists may still want to try it.

To the north of Route 5 are many of the battlegrounds of 1862 and 1864, including Mechanicsville, Seven Pines, Gaines Mill, Beaver Dam Creek, and Cold Harbor. They are indeed worth visiting, but their descriptions are not within the scope of this book.

To the south of Route 5 you'll see signs every few miles for the large number of plantations that have been restored and are open to the public. Every one is worth a visit, but only a few are dealt with here as having direct significance to the military campaigns involving the James River in 1862 and 1864.

Route 5 disappears once you get into Williamsburg, but Route 60 will take you the rest of the scenic way into Newport News.

While there are other, quicker routes to Williamsburg and points on the Chesapeake Bay, this is the historic route—and the only route as far as this author is concerned—by which to travel the Peninsula in order to enjoy the history of the James River.

South of the James, Route 10 roughly parallels the south bank of the river. From it you can visit the battlefields associated with the Bermuda Hundred Campaign, Hopewell and City Point, Windmill Point and Flowerdew Hundred, and other historic sites associated with the Civil War on the way from Petersburg to Portsmouth.

A highly recommended trip is to follow Route 5 out of Richmond, visit the Civil War sites on the north side of the river—including some of the battlegrounds of 1862 and 1864—as well as Williamsburg and Jamestown, take the ferry from Jamestown to Scotland on the south side of the James, then follow Route 10 back to Hopewell and Petersburg. This area of Virginia, however, is so full of history that a week would hardly be enough time to see everything. From the banks of the James on Jamestown Island where Native Americans once fished to the Surry Nuclear Power Plant across the river, five centuries of history can be seen with one sweep of the eye. Many of the sites can be seen in a day, but it is well worth taking the time to do it right.

Of course, seeing some of these sites by boat is also recommended, since, for the most part, that is how many of the Civil War soldiers saw them at least one time or another. There are at least five organized cruises available to tour Hampton Roads, Portsmouth, Norfolk, Newport News, the Naval Bases, Fort Monroe, and Fort Wool. They all last between two and three hours and can give you the viewpoint of hundreds of thousands of Civil War soldiers and sailors of some of the ports so important to strategy in the Civil War in the East.

Launch ramps for private boaters, docking facilities, and overnight marinas are also abundant every few miles along the course of the James. It has been my experience that even on the weekends, the James River is not nearly as busy with small boat traffic as is the Potomac. An overnight cruise up or down the James allowing plenty of time for exploring is encouraged. (Suggested cruises herein are not meant to be used solely for navigational purposes. Always consult current NOS charts and publications, Local Notices to Mariners, and local fishermen or boaters when planning a cruise on any river.)

Notes

1. Dowdey, 59–61.
2. "Robert E. Lee at Fort Monroe," Pamphlet No. 1 in the series *Tales of Old Fort Monroe*.
3. "Fort Monroe in the Civil War," Pamphlet No. 6 in the series *Tales of Old Fort Monroe*.
4. Brig. Gen. R. E. Colston, "Watching the Merrimac," *Battles and Leaders*, Vol. I, 712.
5. Col. John Taylor Wood, C.S.A., "The First Fight of Iron-clads," *Battles & Leaders*, Vol. I, 693–94. "The Monitor and the Merrimack," Pamphlet No. 12 in the series *Tales of Old Fort Monroe*. Sources differ on the angle of the plating on the *Virginia*. A drawing, not necessarily accurate, shows the angle somewhere between thirty-five and forty degrees, but Wood states that the angle was forty-five degrees.
6. Coggins, 133.
7. Sears, 162.
8. As always, figures vary widely and exact numbers are virtually impossible to come by. Stephen Sears (*George B. McClellan: The Young Napoleon*) and Joseph P. Cullen (*The Peninsula Campaign*) disagree on their figures by as much as 50 percent. The point is, McClellan certainly had enough men and supplies, if handled properly, to accomplish his mission. Think of Stonewall Jackson, during the forty-eight-day Valley Campaign, marching nearly seven hundred miles and whipping several different Union commanders in five major battles—all this never with more than 17,000 men.
9. Some excellent insight into the mind of McClellan during the Seven Days' Battles is available in Stephen Sears's *George B. McClellan: The Young Napoleon*, 201–22.
10. Coski, 17.

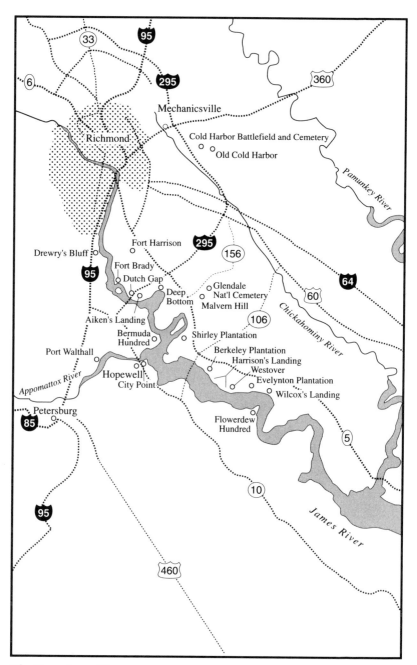

The Upper James River

✦ THE JAMES RIVER: 1864 ✦

I WEIGHED VERY CAREFULLY the advantages and dis-
advantages of moving against Lee's left and moving
against his right. The former promised more decisive
results if immediately successful, and would best prevent
Lee from moving north to make raids, but it would
deprive our army of the advantages of easy communication with a water base of supplies, and compel us
to carry such a large amount of ammunition and rations
in wagon trains, and detach so many troops as train
guards, that I found it presented too many serious
difficulties; and when I considered especially the
sufferings of the wounded in being transported long
distances overland, instead of being carried by short
routes to water, where they could be comfortably
moved by boats, I had no longer any hesitation in
deciding to cross the Rapidan below the position
occupied by Lee's army, and move by our left.[1]

Gen. Ulysses S. Grant was speaking to the eight senior members of
his staff on the night of May 3, 1864, in the small, plain brick house
that served as his headquarters near the railroad station in Culpeper,
Virginia. He had just finished writing some orders, turned his chair
away from the table, crossed his legs, lighted the inevitable cigar, and
summed up what was to become his army's course for the campaigns
that would eventually end the American Civil War.

He added that the movement he outlined would also allow him
to coordinate with Gen. Benjamin F. Butler's Army of the James,
now headed for City Point, at the confluence of the Appomattox

and James rivers. Butler was to approach Richmond from the south side of the James and cut the vital railroad between Richmond and Petersburg. Grant also made it clear that it was Lee's army, and not Richmond or any other Southern city, that was to be the main objective of all of his commanders' efforts. Yet because of Robert E. Lee's determination to keep his army between the Union enemy and his fledgling nation's capital, Grant would necessarily have to operate against Richmond in order to smoke out Lee.

But the most important part of Grant's message had already been conveyed, and the decision to use a water base of supplies, whether he realized it then or not, would result in allowing his army, while invading a hostile country, to subsist there virtually indefinitely. The key to all future operations was securing a river-oriented base of supplies.

The James, the great eastern river that had first sustained the English settlers like a nurturing mother, fed, clothed, armed, comforted, and maintained the armies that would eventually win the Civil War. Grant's decision to make his plans around a water base of supplies would result in a never-ending tide of food, communications, ammunition, and transport of the wounded and their replacements.

And his decision to deny that river to the enemy—or their failure to deny it to him—was as important a step toward eventual Union success as was the Union victory at Gettysburg or the Confederate defeat during the siege of Vicksburg.

Grant would display his tenaciousness in warfare against Robert E. Lee over the next few months. Tactical stalemates at the Wilderness, Spotsylvania, and Cold Harbor would be turned into strategic victories as Grant continually sidestepped the Confederates and continued to press southward. Though his losses after crossing the Rapidan on May 3–4 were reported between 55,000 and 58,000, Grant believed those figures were too high: A man who had been wounded twice and then died would be counted three times in the casualty lists.

While Grant was fighting Lee in the Wilderness at the beginning of May 1864, Union general Benjamin F. Butler was crossing the James to prepare an advance against Richmond and Petersburg from

Bermuda Hundred. That advance was stymied by the Confederates under Gen. P. G. T. Beauregard during several crucial battles around Drewry's Bluff and Fort Stevens.

BERMUDA HUNDRED

WHILE GRANT'S CROSSING OF THE James River on June 14–15, 1864, is the more celebrated passage of the great river, it was made almost a month and a half after Gen. Benjamin F. Butler's landings at City Point and Bermuda Hundred.

After coming from the Western Theater of the Civil War and taking command of all the Union armies, General Grant left Washington on March 31, 1864, and arrived at Fort Monroe the next day to confer with General Butler, who commanded the Army of the James from the fort.

It was supposed to be a short visit, but a severe storm blew up about sunset, just as Grant was about to set sail to return to Washington, and he was forced to remain through April 2. That morning, when he went ashore, General Butler put forth a plan to land a force of Union troops at Bermuda Hundred, an area between a large bend in the James and the confluence of the Appomattox River about five miles wide at its widest and four miles deep from its narrowest point to the James. From this area of land, which could be

BERMUDA HUNDRED IS REACHED from Route 95 south of Richmond. Turn east on Route 10 toward Hopewell. Less than a half mile to the left is the northern end of the "bottleneck," and Route 10 traverses Bermuda Hundred. Route 827 to the left takes you to the Bermuda Hundred Landing on the James. The closest boat launching facilities, should you wish to see both City Point and the Bermuda Hundred Landing from the James, are at the Jordan Point Yacht Haven, accessible from the north side of the James by following Route 5 to Route 156 south, or from the south side by following Route 10 to Route 156 north. Jordan Point Yacht Haven is on the south side of the James.

supported by waterborne transports, Butler proposed to operate against Petersburg and the Confederate capital of Richmond from south of the James.

Strategically, the plan would fit in

with what Grant intended to do north of the James, which was to fight and maneuver General Lee and his Army of Northern Virginia away from Washington, while eventually driving between him and his avenues of supply from the south.

Tactically, the position at Bermuda Hundred was flawed as far as the offensive base it was supposed to provide. Military men of the day on both sides described it as a "bottle," with the Appomattox and James approaching to within about three miles of one another where the "bottle" opened to the west. With Butler's army inside the "bottle," a small Confederate force could build fortifications across the narrow neck of land and keep the Northerners from moving. And after initial Union successes, that is just what happened.

"The James River will never again present such a scene as that of the 5th of May, 1864. An army of forty thousand men afloat on its waters, conveyed by various vessels of the navy, then under command of Admiral Lee."[2] Such was the scene upon the James River as described by Maj. Gen. William F. Smith. He continues describing the flotilla that left Fort Monroe and Newport News and cruised up the James:

It was a motley array of vessels. Coasters and river steamers, ferry-boats and tugs, screw and side-wheel steamers, sloops, schooners, barges, and canal-boats raced or crawled up the stream toward the designated landing. General Butler, to make his own command a perfect unit, improvised for his own purposes a volunteer navy under the command of General C. K. Graham, an ex-navy officer, who, scorning the slow and steady progress of the admiral's squadron, took the lead, followed by the fastest transports in what seemed to be some grand national pageant.[3]

As Smith points out, fortunately the Confederates had not mined the river or placed artillery in hidden positions, or Butler's lightly armed pageant would have been tragically spoiled. By nightfall on May 5, 1864, a landing at Bermuda Hundred had been made.

After securing a defensive line across the narrow part of the "bottle," Butler began his campaign against the Confederate capital and Petersburg on May 6, which would culminate in the Battle of Fort Stevens.

Butler's troops fought a battle at Port Walthall Junction on May 6–7 before they could begin destroying the railroad between Richmond and Petersburg. On May 8 Confederates were repulsed at Swift Creek in their attempt to stop the Federal troops driving south toward Petersburg. On May 9 Butler split his force to drive northward along the railroad and

Richmond and Petersburg Turnpike, stopping that evening a couple miles east of Chester Station.

At 5:15 A.M. on May 10, Confederates attacked the Union troops from the north in an attempt to drive them back to Bermuda Hundred. After fighting most of the day, the Federals were reinforced by troops from the southern wing of their army, and the Confederates withdrew.

On May 11 Butler formulated plans for a general advance toward Richmond to begin the next day. But the Union advance on May 12 was hindered by marshy ground, dense foliage, and a Confederate line firmly entrenched along Proctor's Creek, and it ground to a halt. The men camped for the night in the rain.

Crossing Proctor's Creek took nearly all the following day, but after some heavy fighting on the Union left flank, the Federal forces occupied Woolridge Hill and flanked the Confederates, although the success came too late in the day to exploit.

Skirmishers sent out on the morning of May 14 found that the Confederates had abandoned their defensive lines north of Proctor's Creek, establishing a new line nearer Fort Stevens, with Drewry's Bluff—of 1862 fame—on their extreme left flank.

The next day, Butler made plans to continue the assault. General Smith, anxious about his position, which could be flanked to his right, was given the information that three regiments were in reserve and available to him. Not satisfied that they would still be there when he needed them most, Smith told his commanders in the exposed area to gather up as much telegraph wire as they could and string it between the tree stumps in their front as a makeshift impediment to any assaulting troops.

The trip-wire defenses worked. Confederate general P. G. T. Beauregard had planned an assault on that end of the Union line in order to intercede between the Union Army and the James River, thus hoping to cut the army off from its base of supply and force its surrender. But in the early morning counterattack by the Confederates through a heavy fog, the front lines fell over the unexpected, nearly invisible telegraph wire and, according to General Smith, "were slaughtered like partridges." One of the Union commanders in the area, General Weitzel, wrote that the Rebels were piled in heaps over the telegraph wire and later reported that the Richmond papers called the wire "a devilish contrivance which none but a Yankee could devise," choosing to ignore their own troops' use of land mines (called "subterranean shells") and underwater mines (called torpedoes or "infernal machines"). This was a war that was still fought by rules—

with a good measure of media hypocrisy on both sides—and the use of wire to impede attacking troops, though commonplace during World War I, was still considered unfair trickery.[4]

Beauregard's plan was to include a Confederate force advancing on the Federal rear from the south, but it never materialized. The Confederate victory was incomplete, yet they did drive Butler's troops back into the "bottle," to be neutralized as a fighting force until Grant crossed the James in their support.

By the beginning of June, Grant again had been temporarily stopped by Lee's forces during the fighting at Cold Harbor, his men haunted in the darkness by the poorly interred bones and skulls of comrades who had died in the fighting there two years before. Grant's own casualties of 13,000 would add extensively to this killing ground east of Richmond. ∎

☞ **W H A T · T O · S E E** Bermuda Hundred is a fairly large area, and the battles fought in May 1864 extend any tour of the pertinent sites from the northern outskirts of Petersburg all the way to Drewry's Bluff. An excellent abbreviated tour of most of the sites is available in pamphlet form (for $1.50) from the Chesterfield Historical Society, P.O. Box 40, Chesterfield, VA 23832. The pamphlet includes descriptions of the 1864 battles for Drewry's Bluff, Fort Stevens, the construction of Dutch Gap Canal, Fort Carpenter, Fort Drake, Gen. Benjamin Butler's Headquarters at Cobb's Hill (private property), Point of Rocks Park and associated walking paths, the battles of Port Walthall Junction, Swift Creek, Chester Station, Woolridge Hill, and other sites associated with the Bermuda Hundred Campaign, such as Batteries Dantzler and Wilcox. Most of the sites are accessible by the public but a few are private property or in the development stage.

GRANT CROSSES THE JAMES

ON MAY 26 GRANT SHIFTED HIS BASE of supplies from Port Royal on the Rappahannock River to White House on the Pamunkey River. He had successfully used the Rappahannock to supply his army once he crossed the Rapidan during the fighting in the Wilderness and at Spotsylvania. Driving farther away from that base, he found another base where a railroad terminated at the water. Using the landing at White House, his army could be supplied via the York River, into which the Pamunkey flowed. While he was east of Richmond, White House provided the shortest route for supplies coming up the river.[5]

But after the Battle of Cold Harbor, June 1–3, 1864, Grant decided to avoid the swamps of the Chickahominy River, which had proved a quagmire for McClellan in 1862, and to swing again to the east and south. In a communication with Major General Halleck, Chief of Staff of the Army in Washington, he explained his reasons:

A full survey of all the ground satisfies me that it would be impracticable to hold a line north-east of Richmond that would protect the Fredericksburg Railroad to enable us to use that road for supplying the army. To do so would give us a long vulnerable line of road to protect, exhaust-

WILCOX'S LANDING CAN BE reached from Route 5. Follow the signs at the junction of Routes 5 and 618 taking you south, toward the river on 618. The neck of land in the distance is Windmill Point on the Flowerdew Hundred plantation.

ing much of our strength to guard it, and would leave open to the enemy all of his lines of communication on the south side of the James. . . .

. . . I will move the army to the south side of the James River, either by crossing the Chickahominy and marching near to City Point, or by going to the mouth of the Chickahominy on [the] north side and crossing there.[6]

General Butler had already secured City Point at the beginning of May, and on June 9 Grant directed that all troops arriving at White House be sent on to City Point. At the same time, he sent Colonels Porter and Comstock of his staff to find a suitable crossing point for the Army of the Potomac.

Comstock and Porter had served on General McClellan's staff when it had been on the north bank of the James in the spring and summer of 1862 and were familiar with the area. After thoroughly inspecting several spots, they reported to Grant on June 12 that the best place to cross was the narrowest point on the river below City Point. The river shrank to about half a mile between Wilcox's Landing on the north shore of the James and Windmill Point on the south bank.

Grant had already begun setting things into motion and, according to Porter, seemed more nervous than Porter had ever seen him before. Grant had already ordered his base of supplies shifted from White House to City Point. After Comstock and Porter's report, Grant sent the army marching toward the James that very evening.[7]

Gen. Winfield Hancock's Corps had endured a forced march to reach Wilcox's Landing on the afternoon of June 13 and found Grant waiting for them there. In preparation for the army's crossing, Grant sent word to Butler upriver at Bermuda Hundred to fill several large boats with rocks and sink them in the channel of the James. This would prevent any Confederate gunboats from running down the river from Richmond to shell the Union troops while they were crossing either on ferries or on the pontoon bridges.

Hancock's Corps began ferrying across the river on June 14 and completed the crossing before daylight the next morning. The main crossing point was to be on pontoon bridges stretching almost two thousand feet from Weyanoke Point to the ancient plantation of Flowerdew Hundred. ▪

☛ **W H A T · T O · S E E** Like many of the landings on the James River that once teemed with troops, ships, wagons, horses, and famous officers, Wilcox's Landing (spelled "Willcox's" on the sign pointing to it) has become another nearly forgotten spot along the river's edge. Shortly after the army pulled up its pontoon bridge, local fishermen probably began to use the road cut by engineers to the water as a launching spot for their rowboats and skiffs. The road to the water was recently improved to allow the use of boat trailers. The landing today retains none of its bustling Civil War ambience, and looks more like it probably did just before the Union Army came and went.

FLOWERDEW HUNDRED

THE ENGLISH SETTLEMENTS IN VIR-
ginia were originally based on joint-
stock ventures with charters granted
by King James I. By 1619 a new policy
encouraging private investments had
been instituted. With the new policy,
groups of men or wealthy individuals
could start privately owned settlements, called "particular plantations"
or "hundreds." Sir George Yeardley,
then governor of the colony, took advantage of the changes that gave more
freedom to investors and the sole right
to profits, and he established a settlement that continues as one of the old-
est continuously occupied and farmed
plantations in the country.

Yeardley named the settlement
Flowerdew Hundred after the family
of his wife, Temperance Flowerdew.
His settlement survived the Virginia
massacre by Native Americans in
March 1622—the same massacre that
wiped out the settlement at Wolstenholme Towne (where Carter's Grove
eventually would be built) and numerous other settlements downriver.
Flowerdew Hundred not only survived
the massacre but flourished.

Yeardley sold Flowerdew Hundred
to Abraham Peirsey in 1624, and the
1625 muster showed that fifty-seven
people were living on the plantation,
including twenty-nine servants and
"7 Negroes" working as indentured

FLOWERDEW HUNDRED PLAN-
tation can be reached from
Route 10, or from Route 5 by crossing the James over the Benjamin
Harrison Bridge (Route 156) and
turning left (east) onto Route 10.
After about five miles you will
begin to see signs for Flowerdew
Hundred.

For those boating on the James,
the site of the bridgehead, according to the latest published nautical
chart, is about where buoy "77B"
Fl G 4sec, 15ft is located. No public
docking facilities are available at
Flowerdew Hundred. (Note: This
information is not for navigational
purposes. Always consult current
NOS charts and publications,
Local Notices to Mariners, and
local boaters when planning a
cruise.)

servants. There was a minister, three
single men, and six families and their
servants. On the plantation were
dwelling houses, tobacco barns, storage facilities, and even a windmill.
The windmill was probably used for
grinding corn, which was a product of
Flowerdew Hundred. Peas, hogs, and
cattle were also raised there. The exact
location of the windmill is no longer
known, but the point of land referred

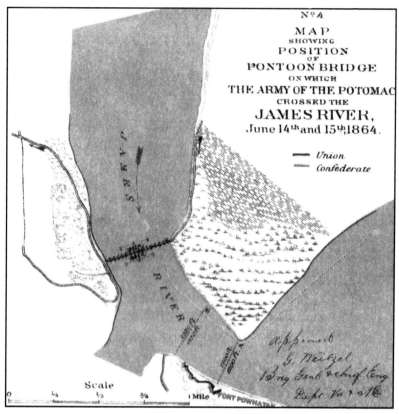

A pontoon bridge connected Weyanoke Point with Flowerdew Hundred.

to by Civil War soldiers as "Windmill Point" has carried that name since the 1670s. Although archaeologists still probe the clay of Flowerdew Hundred, the original site of the windmill, like so many seventeenth-century riverside landmarks, probably was appropriated by the meandering James and now may lie beneath a dozen or so feet of flowing water.

The names of early Virginians have lasted through the centuries, giving a comforting continuity to many of the state's special places. So it is with Wilcox's Landing (or Willcox's Landing) and John Vaughan Willcox, a well-to-do merchant from Petersburg who bought the various segments of the original Flowerdew Hundred tract, reuniting them just before the Civil War. The number of black indentured servants had increased on the Hundred since Governor Yeardley's day, and they raised corn, grain, and of course, tobacco, the cash crop of most ante-bellum plantations in Virginia since the early 1600s.

One site that went undiscovered for nearly a century and a quarter was the location of the bridgehead for the pontoon bridge used by the Union Army when they crossed the James. Union engineers spanned the James from Weyanoke Point, the tongue of land in the large bend in the James, to Flowerdew Hundred with 101 pontoons, set twenty feet apart and secured to schooners anchored upstream in the channel. Planks were laid edge-to-edge to provide a roadway eleven feet wide and nearly two thousand feet long, with a re-movable section in the center to allow for river traffic. Perhaps the most amazing thing about it was that it was completed in seven hours.[8]

At 1:00 A.M. on June 15 began a procession hardly surpassed in war-fare. The following is from General Porter's account:

As the general-in-chief [Grant] stood upon the bluff on the north bank of the river on the morning of June 15, watch-ing with unusual interest the busy scene spread out before him, it presented a sight which had never been equalled even in his extended experience in all the varied phases of warfare. His cigar had been thrown aside, his hands were clasped behind him, and he seemed lost in the contemplation of the spectacle. The great bridge was the scene of continuous movement of infantry columns, batteries of artillery, and wagon trains. The approaches to the river on both banks were covered with masses of troops mov-ing briskly to their positions or waiting patiently for their turn to cross. At the two improvised ferries steamboats were gliding back and forth with the regularity of weavers' shuttles. A fleet of transports covered the surface of the water below the bridge, and gunboats floated lazily upon the stream, guarding the river above. Drums were beating the march, bands were playing stirring quicksteps, the distant booming of cannon . . . the cheers of the sailors, the shouting of the troops, the rumbling of wheels, the shrieks of the steam whistles. The bright sun, shining through a clear sky upon the scene, cast its sheen upon the water, was reflected from the burnished gun-barrels and glittering cannon, and brought out with increased brilliancy the gay colors of the waving banners. . . . The rich grain was standing high in the surrounding fields. The harvest was almost ripe, but the harvesters had fled. The arts of civi-lization had recoiled before the science of destruction; and in looking from the growing crops to the marching columns, the gentle smile of peace contrasted strangely with the savage frown of war. It was a matchless pageant that could not fail to inspire all beholders with the grandeur of achievement and the majesty of military power. The man whose genius had conceived and whose skill had *executed this masterly movement stood watching the spectacle in profound silence. . . .*[9]

A Confederate general writing after the war described the bridge with a little more brevity, but no less majestically when he said it was "the greatest . . . the world has seen since the days of Xerxes."[10]

For seventy hours, 60,000 men and a wagon train of supplies, ambulances, and artillery, estimated to be between fifty and sixty miles long, crossed the bridge. By early morning of June 18, the bridge was dismantled. Over the years, as the river ebbed and flowed, the bridgehead vanished.

In 1986 archaeologist Taft Kiser took a Civil War–era photograph by Brady & Company to a site shown on a Civil War–era map done for a report by Brig. Gen. Godfrey Weitzel, chief engineer for the bridge project. There Kiser discovered an old cypress tree similar to one prominent in the June 15, 1864, photo. Simultaneously, in California, Flowerdew Hundred research associate Gene Prince was developing the technique—later to be named after him—of putting a slide of an old photo into a camera's viewfinder and locating a historic site by aligning the image with existing landscape features. In the summer of 1986, Kiser and Prince combined their two methods of visual archaeology and determined the site of the pontoon bridgehead. After 122 years, the James surrendered one of its innumerable secrets.[11] ∎

☛ **W H A T · T O · S E E** Flowerdew Hundred is one of the best-preserved seventeenth-century English settlements in America, and it has yielded a treasury of archaeological information. Archaeologists have located more than sixty sites dating from prehistory to the present—from Native American villages over eleven thousand years old to a dozen early colonists' settlements, one of which was an enclosed village with wooden buildings and a large dwelling complex. Hundreds of artifacts including glass beads, pipes, armor, gun parts, tools, and pottery have been uncovered, and other sites have yet to be explored.[12]

Weyanoke Point is on private land, and access to the northern bridgehead site is restricted. Flowerdew Hundred is also privately owned but is open to the public, and it offers tours, including a walk down to the bridgehead site. Admission is charged. For more information, contact The Flowerdew Hundred Foundation, 1617 Flowerdew Hundred Road, Hopewell, VA 23860, telephone (804) 541-8897 or (804) 541-8938.

A railroad once ran under this bluff at City Point, carrying cargo to thousands of Union soldiers.

CITY POINT

AFTER WATCHING THE MAGNIFICENT procession of his army crossing the James, Grant procured a ferryboat and had his headquarters staff ferried across the river. From the south side of the James, he rode to City Point to establish permanent headquarters there.

Before the war, City Point was just a tiny port village located where the Appomattox River flows into the James. But this sleepy Virginia riverfront town became one of the busiest ports in the world after Grant moved

CITY POINT IS LOCATED ON THE north end of Hopewell, Virginia. Signs to Hopewell are visible on Virginia Route 10, and once in Hopewell, additional signs direct you to the City Point Unit of the Petersburg National Battlefield. For boaters, City Point is at the confluence of the James and Appomattox rivers just upstream of buoy "118" Fl R 4sec. The large Eppes Mansion is a good landmark.

City Point during the Civil War

his supply base there. The City Point Railroad, which ran from the docks on the James to Petersburg, about eight miles away, by mid-June was running directly into the rear of the Union lines outside of Petersburg. An estimated fifteen hundred tons of supplies a day were being off-loaded from transports that steamed in and out from the half mile of wharf along the James. Several railroad siding tracks were filled with boxcars and locomotives. Once loaded, they huffed their way directly to the army in the trenches at Petersburg. What wasn't transported immediately was stored in warehouses built along the river's shore, and on any one day the Union Army could count nine million meals for the soldiers and twelve thousand tons of fodder for the animals. Bread was baked daily at City Point: one hundred thousand rations each day.

Barges made trips down the Potomac from Washington and up the James bringing 275 railroad cars and twenty-five engines. In just over three weeks, engineers and pioneers finished the first part of the railroad. Thereafter, trains ran on a full schedule.

The town had stables, camps, sutlers' shacks, storehouses, a post office, a chapel, a rectory, a telegraph office, and provost marshal's and quartermaster's department offices. The U.S. Christian Commission also had an office at City Point.

City Point was a natural funnel for

Confederate prisoners being herded north to more permanent prison camps. Transports ascending the James to City Point in the last two weeks of the war carted off some 14,000 rebel prisoners. Some of the more noteworthy were Gen. Joseph B. Kershaw, Gen. Richard S. Ewell, and Gen. G. W. Custis Lee, son of the commanding general of all the Confederate armies, Robert E. Lee.

A fenced-in, open area called the "Bull Ring" was used as a prison for those suspected of crimes perpetrated while in the army. Without adequate shelter and sanitary facilities, the Bull Ring gained a reputation as odious as the stench it emitted.

City Point's hospital facilities, on the other hand, were regarded as some of the finest in the country. The Depot Field Hospital was the largest of seven, with a capacity for 10,000 sick and wounded men. Log barracks kept the patients warm in the winter, and covered walkways and twelve hundred tents kept them comfortable in the summer heat. U.S. Sanitary and Christian Commission workers helped the male nurses and army surgeons who administered the hospital. Though the fighting and trenches around Petersburg continued to create misery for the soldiers, when they were evacuated to City Point they could expect to receive some of the finest treatment in the country.

Additionally, because it was chosen

by Grant as his headquarters, it was also the nerve center in the field for the entire Federal war effort from June 22, 1864, until the siegelines around Petersburg were broken in April 1865. President Abraham Lincoln visited City Point by riverboat twice to discuss the war strategy with Grant. Grant issued orders for Union forces operating in the Shenandoah Valley, Georgia, Maryland, Tennessee, North Carolina, South Carolina, Alabama, and of course, for the siege operations tightening around Petersburg, all from his headquarters at City Point.[13]

As the summer of 1864 wore on, City Point grew in importance and in size as a depot for the Union forces in Virginia. Along with the tons of food, clothing, hospital supplies, and arms stockpiled, there were also tons of ammunition waiting at City Point at any one time to be distributed to the soldiers in the field. A single ship loaded with ammunition was a floating powder keg. Tied up at the wharf, it had all the potential to destroy huge quantities of supplies and perhaps to kill or injure some of the higher-ranking officers in the Union Army, including Grant himself.

Union officers, in particular the assistant provost marshal General Sharpe, thought there were a number of Confederate spies roaming about at City Point. On August 9, 1864, at about 11:40 A.M., Sharpe had just

finished telling Grant, who was sitting before his tent, of his convictions about the spies and a plan to discover and capture them. He had no sooner left Grant when a tremendous explosion shook the earth beneath them. A rain of deadly debris came down—bullets, shells, boards, pieces of wood—killing a number of horses and an orderly and wounding a member of Grant's staff and three orderlies. Grant was not only unhurt but unruffled. He didn't even rise from his chair to go to the bluff to see what had blown up, and within five minutes he was writing a report about the incident. Horace Porter ran, with the rest of the staff, to the bluff and discovered that a boat loaded with ordnance had exploded, killing forty-three and wounding another forty.

Porter was appointed head of a board to determine the cause of the explosion. At the time they reported that it was the mishandling of ammunition by laborers on the boat that caused the explosion, but most had a suspicion that the Confederates had something to do with it.

It wasn't until several years after the war, when Porter was working for the Grant administration, that he discovered the true nature of that explosion. A Virginian had come to the White House to complain about a patent. In explaining his experience as an inventor to Porter, he told him of an "infernal machine" he had once created

Grant spent the winter of 1864–65 at this cabin at City Point.

that was an explosive device detonated by a clock mechanism: a time bomb. He explained that to prove his device worked, he had sneaked into the Union depot at City Point disguised as a laborer, planted the bomb on an ammunition boat, and set the clock for a half hour so that he could escape. Porter not only was finally enlightened as to the nature of the great explosion at City Point but also admitted to the Virginian that he knew—firsthand since the explosion had come close to killing him—that the man had remarkable skill as an inventor.[14]

The importance of City Point continued to grow over the next several months, and the Confederates would have another opportunity—this time using ironclad warships—to attempt to destroy the nerve center of

the Union war effort at the confluence of the James and Appomattox rivers.

In January 1865 a peace commission consisting of Confederate vice president Alexander Stephens, Confederate senator Robert Hunter, and assistant Confederate secretary of war John Campbell used City Point to pass through the Union lines and speak with President Abraham Lincoln and Secretary of State Seward concerning a negotiated peace between the two sections of the country. Their meeting was held at Hampton Roads, Virginia, on the *River Queen*. According to Grant, Lincoln had said to the peace commissioners that he was willing to sign his name to a blank piece of paper and that the Confederates could fill in the terms of surrender, as long as they agreed on two points: that the

Union be preserved and that slavery be abolished. Needless to say, negotiations hung up on both issues, the major one being Southern independence, so the diminutive Stephens and his commission returned disappointed to Richmond via City Point.

During the visit of the peace commissioners, Stephens, a tiny man, looked very large in the dusk as he and his group boarded the *Mary Martin*, a Hudson riverboat outfitted for passengers and stationed on the James River at City Point. He looked so massive because of his bulky, coarse wool overcoat, common in the South since the beginning of the war. The coat was apparently even thicker than normal and reached almost to Stephens's feet. When Stephens removed the coat, Grant noticed a radical change in the man's size.

Shortly after the peace commissioners left, Grant and Lincoln were discussing the meeting between the Confederate representatives and the president. After a few minutes, Lincoln suddenly asked Grant if he had seen that overcoat of Stephens. Grant answered in the affirmative. "Well," Lincoln said, "did you see him take it off?" Grant said he had. "Well," Lincoln said, "didn't you think it was the biggest shuck and the littlest ear that ever you did see?"[15]

Lincoln visited City Point in June 1864 and again in March 1865 and stayed for almost two weeks during his last trip aboard the *River Queen*, anchored off the point. He visited the camps at City Point, speaking with junior officers and a large number of wounded men in the hospital. Coming upon a group of soldiers cutting timber, the president hoisted an ax and began hacking away at a log while the men gave him a hearty hurrah. ∎

☛ **W H A T · T O · S E E** The National Park Service recently acquired the City Point area and is in the process of restoring much of the headquarters site as well as providing information on the other important historic spots to see. Almost everything at City Point is within walking distance from the Visitor Center in the Eppes House. Grant's original winter cabin rests close to the same foundation where it was when he and his family spent the winter of 1864–65 there. A walk around the gardens and down to the shore below the City Point bluff emphasizes how fleeting history can be: Where wharves and railroad track once carried cargo enough to satisfy the demands of an entire army at war, nothing is left but the sandy shore and the water of the James.

DEEP BOTTOM

GRANT SWIFTLY SIDESTEPPED LEE after the battles in the Wilderness, at Spotsylvania, and at Cold Harbor, then rapidly crossed the James, but his expectations of capturing Petersburg drew up short because of a mix-up in orders. According to Grant's memoirs, because General Meade did not pass on his orders to General Hancock that once Hancock crossed the James he was to advance on Petersburg, precious time was lost in attacking that city. As it was, Union soldiers captured the outer earthworks, but by June 18, 1864, their attacks stalled against an inner Confederate line bolstered by Confederate reinforcements.[16]

On Tuesday, June 21, 1864, the same day that President Lincoln arrived at City Point to confer with Grant and review the army, Grant had ordered Gen. Benjamin Butler to build a pontoon bridge across the James River at Deep Bottom to facilitate and secure supply and communications between Union forces still north of the James now that both Butler's and Grant's troops were south of the river. (Though much has been made of Butler's troops being "bottled up" in the area of land between the James and the Appomattox rivers known as Bermuda Hundred, the ease with which he built this pontoon bridge and others and the continuing flow of

DEEP BOTTOM IS REACHED from Route 5. About nine miles outside of the Richmond city limits, watch for Kingsland Road on the right. Turn right on Kingsland, travel about one-half mile, and turn left on Deep Bottom Road. Follow it to the end at the river. Jones Neck is the land visible opposite the modern launch ramp that descends into the river at virtually the same spot the pontoon bridge was anchored.[19] Jones Neck, because of a canal through the bottom of the neck called the Jones Neck Cutoff, is now inaccessible except by boat. The river around Jones Neck appears navigable, from buoy "144" Fl R 4s PA on the downriver side of the neck at Jones Neck Cutoff, around the big loop in the river the Neck makes, to buoy "146" Fl R 4sec at the upriver end of Jones Neck Cutoff. Use caution when approaching buoy "146" to avoid "Woodson's Rock," shallow water, and a snag close to the buoy. (Note: These directions are not intended for navigational purposes. Consult current NOS charts and publications, Local Notices to Mariners, and local boaters before cruising these waters.)

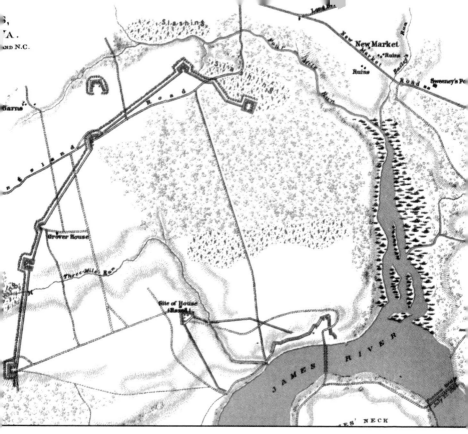

Union defensive lines at Deep Bottom in October 1864

supplies to him from the James River at Bermuda Hundred Landing indicate that the "bottle" was hardly as tightly corked as one is led to believe.)

The next day, Lincoln's river steamer left City Point, stopped at Bermuda Hundred Landing to pick up General Butler and at Admiral Lee's flagship to bring the admiral aboard, and traveled up the James to observe the fortifications seen from the river. The pontoon bridge at Deep Bottom had been constructed, like most of the permanent pontoon bridges, with a removable center sec-

tion for river traffic. Orders went up the river to have it removed for the passage of the president. Lincoln's steamer passed through the bridge and went some distance up the river, then returned later to City Point.[17]

The pontoon bridge across the James at Deep Bottom—as well as another constructed just downstream—was the scene of an example of Grant's ingenuity in military subterfuge. In July 1864 the Union Army was preparing to explode several tons of powder below the Confederate entrenchments at Petersburg in a mine soldiers from the 48th Pennsylvania Regiment had dug. Grant wanted to make a feint against Richmond on the north side of the James to draw some of Lee's army out of the Petersburg lines. On the afternoon of July 26, Hancock's Corps was pulled from its position and made a quick march to Deep Bottom north of the James. This was followed by Philip Sheridan's Union cavalry.

By 3:30 P.M. on July 27, Lee was sending troops hurriedly to the north side of the James, anticipating a rush on Richmond. Sheridan made a move on Lee's left flank and was attacked by Lee's veterans. Sheridan drove the Confederates back, capturing some 250 prisoners in the Battle of Darby-town. Lee no doubt by now was convinced that Grant was attempting to take Richmond.

The mine explosion and subsequent assault were planned for the early morning hours of July 30. To give the impression he was continuing his attack on Richmond, Grant had all artillery firing in front of Petersburg halted and the guns hidden. Sheridan, to muffle the sound of his horses' hooves, covered a second pontoon bridge with dirt, grass, and moss. This bridge was constructed at Deep Bottom about one-half mile down-stream (about where the river dis-appears around the bend). Sheridan then moved his division to the south side of the James. There he dis-mounted his men, left his horses, and marched his troopers in daylight—this time posing as infantry reinforce-ments moving north of the James—under the watchful eyes of the Con-federates, to convince them even further that Grant was bringing more troops up to attack Richmond instead of Petersburg. Grant brought a wagon train across the bridge—empty, of course—to continue the ruse.

Transports, tugs, and steamers were sailed up the river, whistles shrieking

---

☛ **W H A T · T O · S E E** The scene of Grant's great military ruse at the end of July 1864 is now just a modern launch site for fishing and recreation on the James. According to Civil War maps, this is the site of one of the pontoon bridges across the James to Jones Neck. The other was located downstream at the bend of the river and could at least be seen partially from this spot. Watching the James flow by this quiet site, it is easy to imagine the river steamer with Abraham Lincoln and his party rounding the big bend to your left and plowing its way through the opened center section of the bridge. It is also easy to imagine the racket raised by the steamers and trans-ports ordered here by Grant to trick the Confederates into believing an attack on Richmond was imminent.

and running lights burning, as if they were carting more troops and supplies to the north bank of the river. Then, under cover of darkness on July 29, Hancock suddenly pulled his divisions out of the lines before Richmond and marched them fifteen miles to the south side of the James to a point in support of Burnside's Union Corps. This corps was to stage the assault after the mine explosion tore a gap in the Confederate lines at Petersburg.

The explosion ripped a crater 170 feet long and 30 feet deep in the Confederate lines, but the Union assault failed, and the siege of Petersburg would go on until the next spring. The event was summed up by Horace Porter: "Thus ended an operation conceived with rare ingenuity, prepared with unusual forethought, and executed up to the moment of the final assault with consummate skill, and which yet resulted in absolute failure from sheer incapacity on the part of subordinates." [18]

The Deep Bottom crossing would be used later that summer and into the fall as a vital link between the segments of the Union Army north and south of the James. By October 26, extensive earthworks would be thrown up extending over three thousand yards. [19] ∎

AIKEN'S LANDING

AIKEN'S LANDING, NAMED AFTER ITS owner and also known as Varina, was the site of a 1350-foot bridge that was made the subject of a detailed illustration by Lt. W. R. King, acting chief of engineers in the Union Army's Department of Virginia. The drawing was done in January 1865, and the bridge was one that probably replaced or accompanied the original 1320-foot pontoon bridge that spanned the river where Varina Road struck it. Mr. Aiken's loyalty to the Union was nonexistent, and he continued to aid the Confederate cause even after promising the Federal forces demanding

AIKEN'S LANDING IS ON PRIVATE land and inaccessible, but the river there is navigable between buoy "147" Fl G 4sec 16ft at the eastern end of the Jones Neck Cutoff and buoy "150" Fl R 4sec 18ft. The pontoon bridge, according to historian William Frassanito, was anchored about six hundred yards downriver from the Aiken house. [20] (Not for navigational purposes. Consult NOS charts and publications, Local Notices to Mariners, and local boaters before cruising this area.)

☛ **W H A T · T O · S E E** The Aiken House is privately owned and has been altered somewhat from its original Civil War appearance, yet it retains some of the rural James riverfront ambience of many of the homes along the river. Please respect the privacy of the current owners.

---

compliance that he would not. He spent some time incarcerated in Fort Monroe for that, and when the U.S. government wrested away his plantation permanently from Confederates at the end of September 1864, Aiken's Landing would provide one more exit for Union forces from the so-called "bottle," from which they could advance toward the ever-lengthening Confederate lines. ∎

FORT HARRISON

UNION GENERALS ORD AND BIRNEY crossed the James at Deep Bottom on September 28, 1864, and the next day launched a two-pronged attack against the Confederate lines outside Richmond on the north side of the James. Birney and his 10th Corps attacked the Confederate fort on the New Market Road north of Fort Harrison, and Ord's 18th Corps captured Fort Harrison.

Grant was with Birney and had an unwelcome aide-de-camp accompany him during the battle. His youngest son, Jesse, had traveled along with him on the riverboat from City Point. The six-year-old had brought along his black Shetland pony, Little Reb. Jesse rode with the general and his staff until the bullets started to sing. According to Horace Porter, of Grant's staff,

FORT HARRISON IS PART OF THE National Park Service's Richmond National Battlefield. It can be reached by traveling southeast on Virginia Route 5 about five miles from the Richmond city limits. The battlefield road is on the right and is marked by the park sign. While Fort Harrison may seem rather far from the James River, its capture led to the construction of Fort Brady at the edge of the James.

Grant immediately became involved in directing the battle. Grant was known for his coolness under direct fire, issuing orders or writing dispatches while others ducked and dodged the bullets and shells. As the bullets began whipping the dust around the group, Grant continued in his cool manner until he saw his six-year-old with the group. "What's that youngster doing there?" he shouted and immediately ordered an aide to remove him. Apparently the boy had inherited his father's disdain for enemy bullets and had to be led by the pony's bridle to safety in the rear.

Grant inspected Fort Harrison after it had fallen. He rode up to the ditch before it and dismounted. Walking into the fort, he had to step over and around many of the dead. Some have called Grant a butcher, but Porter described his expression as one of profound grief at the loss of life. Several times while walking into the fort he averted his eyes from the hideously mutilated dead as he passed them. From the north parapet, Grant could just make out the church spires of Richmond. While the Confederates continued to shell the fort, Grant sat cross-legged on the ground and wrote a dispatch. A shell burst almost directly overhead, scattering his aides, but Grant never stopped writing. Porter, who saw the dispatch, said Grant's handwriting didn't even waver the moment the shell burst.

An assault by Lee's troops on Fort Harrison the next day was driven off, and Fort Harrison remained in Federal hands. Union forces now held lines stretching nearly five miles from the bluffs overlooking the James all the way to the New Market Road. ▪

☛ **W H A T · T O · S E E** The Richmond National Battlefield Park road runs from Route 5 south past many of the forts fought over in 1864. Several miles of earthworks are still visible along the park road, including the twelve-foot-deep remnant of what was once a twenty-seven-foot-deep trench. The trench was dug by Confederates in Fort Johnson to keep Federal troops in Fort Harrison from tunneling underneath them and planting a mine like the one used at Petersburg. There is a National Park Service Visitor Center and bookstore at Fort Harrison, with exhibits, walking tours (during the summer season), and information.

FORT BRADY

BY MID-OCTOBER 1864, ON THE BLUFF over the James, Union engineers had completed Fort Brady, and the 1st Connecticut Heavy Artillery had their huge guns in place to shell any Confederate naval squadron attempting to run downriver from Richmond. Over the next several months, soldiers at the fort guarded the James, engaged Confederate artillery across the river, and fired upon boats that ventured too close to the fort.

In January 1865 the Confederate's James River Squadron (not to be confused with the Federal's James River Flotilla) ran past Fort Brady at night while the fort's guns bellowed above them. The Confederates did little damage once they got downriver (see "The *Onondaga* Fiasco") and returned again under the fire of Fort Brady's heavy artillery. Though the squadron's mission failed, it did accomplish two things. First, it emphasized the drawbacks of fixed fortifications: As war

FORT BRADY IS PART OF THE Richmond National Battlefield Park and is reached by automobile from Virginia Route 5 by following the park roads and signs. For boaters, the main channel of the James cuts off the two-mile loop of the river that runs below Fort Brady, and the loop is unmarked. Charts show that the water in the loop is at least eight feet deep, but the channel is very narrow. If you intend to see Fort Brady from the river, please check with local boaters as to its accessibility. (Note: Not intended for navigational purposes. Always consult NOS charts and publications, Local Notices to Mariners, and local boaters before attempting to cruise this section of the river.)

became more mechanical—now with steam-powered boats, then with

☛ **W H A T · T O · S E E** The earthworks at Fort Brady, at the end of the National Park Service road, are in a fine state of preservation, and the interior of the fort can be explored by following posted markers. A Civil War photograph exhibit, placed on the spot where the photographer stood, gives an impressive look into the past. Fort Brady was built by Union engineers to overlook the James River and prevent Confederate gunboats from running down the river. Because of summer foliage, the James can barely be seen below the bluff outside of Fort Brady.

mechanized land warfare in the next century—emplaced heavy artillery pointing in one direction was useless once the swiftly moving mechanized force had passed by. Second, the January raid made the Union Navy realize that their gunboats, steamers, and supply ships were not invulnerable and that the James was still a contested waterway. ∎

TRENT'S REACH, Battery Dantzler, and the Dutch Gap Canal

THE CONFEDERATE "CORK" TO GENERAL Butler's Bermuda Hundred "bottle" was known as the Howlett Line, and it stretched across the narrow neck between the Appomattox River on the south to the bottom of the loop of the James that created Farrar's Island. At the north end of the Howlett Line was Battery Dantzler, named after a Confederate colonel who was killed in an assault on the Union lines in June 1864. Battery Dantzler overlooked a stretch of the James called Trent's Reach, and like Fort Darling at Drewry's Bluff farther up the river, it defended Richmond from any Union gunboats running up the river.

As part of Grant's plan to protect his army while it crossed the James on June 15, 1864, he had ordered General Butler on June 13 to sink some ships as far up the river as he could while still being able to guard them from removal by the enemy. Butler sank some boats in about the middle of Trent's Reach,

THE ENTIRE LOOP NO LONGER exists, so any shallow-draft vessel exploring this section of the James will probably have to turn around and retrace its course. Farrar's Island has a small, shallow lake in the middle of it (with three wrecks—ominous, at best) accessible by a very narrow channel. Unfortunately, as of this writing, Battery Dantzler is not open to the public, and the area looks inaccessible by water. Dutch Gap Canal is now the main channel of the James and is navigable. The old canal begins at buoy "151" Qk Fl G and ends about 175 yards beyond that, before you reach buoy "152" Fl R 4sec. (Note: This is not for navigational purposes. Consult NOS charts and publications, Local Notices to Mariners, and local boaters before attempting to cruise this section of the river.)

the southernmost loop of the James around Farrar's Island. These obstructions would, with one exception, hold the three Confederate ironclads stationed upriver from a foray through the center of the Union lines.

The situation led to a stalemate for both sides, however. General Butler, whom Porter described as being "always fertile in ideas," came up with a plan to negate the effectiveness of Battery Dantzler and avoid his own obstructions in Trent's Reach by changing the course of the James River.

At the northern end of Butler's "bottleneck," the James took a wild loop of almost five miles around Farrar's Island. At the top of the loop, the distance between the two riverbanks was only 174 yards. Butler decided that a canal could be excavated across that narrow neck of land, thus bypassing Trent's Reach and Battery Dantzler.

On August 10, 1864, construction began on what would be called the Dutch Gap Canal. Under frequent fire from sharpshooters and artillery, Union soldiers moved an estimated fifteen thousand cubic yards of earth by hand, in addition to the soil and rocks removed by steam dredges. Work on the canal went on for four and a half months before the bulkhead at the west end of the immense ditch was ready to be blown up. Historian William Frassanito points out that the canal actually was ready to be opened in mid-November, but the Union Navy was concerned that if the canal was opened so that they could proceed upriver, there would be nothing to stop the Confederates from sending their three ironclads downriver.[21] After six weeks of haggling, Butler invited Grant to witness the explosion on New Year's Day 1865, but Grant declined. It was probably a good thing, too. The blast threw thousands of tons of dirt in the air, only to have it fall back into the freshly dug canal. It wouldn't be until after the war that the canal would be serviceable. ∎

☛ **W H A T · T O · S E E** The big southern loop in the James around Farrar's Island has become mostly backwater, in part because of the debris left in Trent's Reach from Butler's obstructions and the shoaling it has caused. Also, after the Dutch Gap Canal was completed, it became the main channel and the loop was no longer maintained. Contemporary charts show pilings, wrecks, and only about three feet of water before the old channel that used to be Trent's Reach becomes of variable depth and swampy.

THE *ONONDAGA* FIASCO

IN MID-JANUARY 1865 GRANT planned an attack on Fort Fisher in North Carolina. Admiral Porter accordingly took most of the ships from the James River to bolster his fleet outside the fort. He was confident that by leaving the double-turreted, monitor-class ironclad USS *Onondaga* and three or four small gunboats, the James could be effectively blocked in Trent's Reach below the obstructions Butler had placed in the river there. The powerful *Onondaga* was commanded by Capt. William A. Parker and boasted two fifteen-inch smoothbore cannons and two 150-pound Parrott rifles, weaponry that was certainly equal to anything the Confederates could put on the river.

The night of January 23, 1865, was exceedingly dark. Suddenly, along the sable ribbon of river above Fort Brady, three Confederate ironclads and, according to Horace Porter, three other gunboats steamed by. The soldiers at Fort Brady fired the large guns until the boats had run past them; then they were unable to swing the huge mounted cannons enough to follow the boats' course downriver. The boats, along with Southern batteries across the river, returned the fire.

In the meantime, Grant at City Point had sent a naval officer up the James to place torpedoes (Civil War–era terminology for underwater mines) at the obstructions at Trent's Reach. By chance, the officer had gone up the same night and discovered the Confederates making their way down the river. By 1:00 A.M. the *Fredericksburg*, the Confederate ironclad with the shallowest draft, had found its way through the obstructions at Trent's Reach. Returning for the other two Rebel ironclads, the commander of the *Fredericksburg* found the *Virginia II* and the *Richmond* aground and the water in the James at ebb tide. By then the alarm had spread and Union artillerists had opened fire on the stranded ironclads and their protectors. With daybreak, Federal artillery became more accurate, destroying one of the smaller ships accompanying the ironclads.

Hearing of the Confederates' penetration down the James, Captain Parker withdrew the *Onondaga,* which was the last Union ironclad between the three Confederate ironclads and City Point. It was probably a wise move. Surprised by the night attack, he no doubt wanted to size up the situation and pick his own part of the river upon which to do battle.

Earlier in the evening, according to Horace Porter, Grant had been informed that at about 10:30 P.M., the Confederate squadron had passed the upper end of the loop around Farrar's Island. They still had to pass the obstructions at Trent's Reach and the formidable *Onondaga.* At 1:00 A.M. he was awakened and told that the Rebel ironclads had passed the obstructions and were headed downriver.

It is difficult to overemphasize City Point's importance to the Union effort at this stage of the war. Tons of rations and ammunition were stockpiled there; miles of rolling stock were running in and out; hundreds of wooden ships were coming and going at the wharves; and the commander of all the Union armies had the web of his communications network anchored at City Point. To add to Grant's wor-

The twin-turreted Onondaga

ries, his wife had come to City Point for the winter and was there when he was told the news.

According to Porter, during a break in the briefing she asked quietly, "Ulyss, will those gunboats shell the bluff?" The general expressed his opinion that they probably would be engaged in fighting the batteries ashore and the gunboats. And of course, the mighty *Onondaga* was there to engage the Rebels in defense of City Point. At that moment, the news came in that the *Onondaga* had withdrawn from the enemy without firing a shot, to below the pontoon bridge. It is not known how Grant would have reacted had his wife not been there. As it was, he exploded in indignation that the captain of such a fine vessel as the *Onondaga* would turn tail and run.

Two hours later the reports were that only one of the ironclads had made it past the obstructions and the others were apparently aground. Union shore batteries had been reinforced.

This waterborne attempt upon City Point by the Confederates was a tremendous strategy—one that may have changed the course of the war if it had succeeded. Opening the James to below City Point with ironclads and gunboats and then obstructing the river there would have split Grant's army into three parts: the army north of the James, Butler's army south of it, and the army and navy of supply below City Point, which was sustaining the Union war effort in Virginia.

 ˙ The *Onondaga* finally sailed upriver, but not until 11:00 the next morning. By then Captain Parker's career as a naval officer was damaged beyond repair. The *Onondaga* lobbed a few shells at the Confederate ironclads, but the tide on the James by then was rising, and the Confederate ships moved out of range. At 9:00 P.M. the Confederates were about to make another attempt, but the *Virginia* had been damaged, and steam and smoke were pouring into her, obstructing the vision of the pilots and gunners. A council of war was held, and though two of the three ironclads were in running order, the attack was canceled. Had they attacked, they would have had to contend only with the *Onondaga* and a few wooden gunboats: two ironclads versus one. As historian William N. Still, Jr., pointed out in his book *Iron Afloat: The Story of the Confederate Armorclads*, "The Confederates certainly had a passing chance of success, and the rewards would have more than justified the odds. The destruction of the enormous supply depot at City Point could have seriously affected Grant's campaign."[22]

As it was, the ill-fated attack by the James River Squadron was the last serious effort by the Confederate Navy on the James River.

Notes

1. Porter, 36–37. The syntax seems rather stiff for Grant speaking unofficially to his officers. Porter no doubt reconstructed what Grant said to the best his memory would serve. We must be satisfied that the fundamental facts attributed to Grant's speech that evening are correct.
2. Maj. Gen. William F. Smith, "Butler's Attack on Drewry's Bluff," *Battles and Leaders*, Vol. 4, 207.
3. *Ibid.*
4. *Ibid.*, 212.
5. Grant, Vol. II, 252–53.
6. *Ibid.*, 279–81n.
7. Porter, 188–90.
8. Frassanito, *Grant and Lee*, 207.
9. Porter, 199–200.
10. Gen. E. P. Alexander, quoted in the pamphlet *Flowerdew Hundred*, published by the Flowerdew Hundred Foundation.
11. Informational pamphlets *The Crossing of the James, Flowerdew Hundred,* and *The Flowerdew Hundred Windmill*, published
by the Flowerdew Hundred Foundation.
12. *Flowerdew Hundred*, pamphlet published by the Flowerdew Hundred Foundation.
13. Grant, 344–76.
14. Porter, 273–75.
15. Grant, 422–23.
16. Grant seemed to blame Meade in his 1885 memoirs, but Horace Porter, in his memoirs published in 1897, said that Hancock, fearful of getting blamed for tardiness, asked for an investigation. According to Porter, Grant assured both Hancock and Meade that no investigation was needed. He subsequently promoted both of them to major general in the regular army, seemingly as a vote of confidence.
17. Porter, 222–23.
18. *Ibid.*, 268–69.
19. *O.R.'s Atlas*, Pl. LXV, 6.
20. Frassanito, *Grant and Lee*, 310.
21. *Ibid.*, 321.
22. Still, 185.

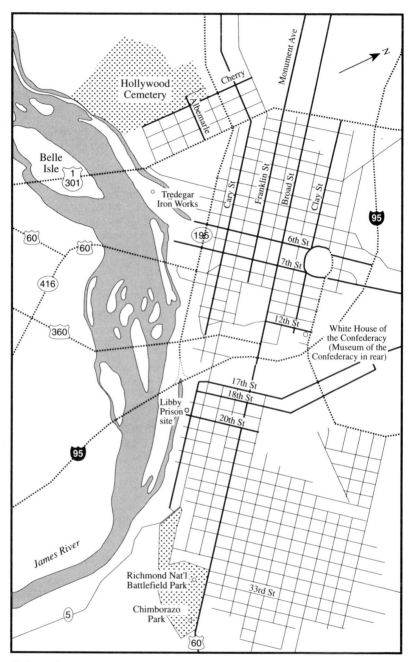

Richmond

✦ THE CONFEDERATE ✦ CAPITAL

ON MARCH 27 AND 28, 1865, aboard the *River Queen*, Lincoln hosted Sherman, Adm. David Porter, and Grant and discussed surrender terms for the Confederates. This meeting would come back to haunt Sherman after Lincoln's death when he had cornered Joseph E. Johnston's army near Durham, North Carolina, on April 17, 1865. Following Grant's lenient surrender demands of Lee's army at Appomattox, and knowing that Lincoln was willing to agree to everything but Confederate independence and the continuation of slavery, Sherman went beyond accepting the unconditional surrender of Johnston's army and wrote up a plan for peace between the two sections. When the more radical Republicans in the North read the agreement, they were incensed. It included the provision that after the Confederate forces were disbanded, they were to deposit their weapons in their own state arsenals. It also went on to declare, among other things, that the president of the United States would recognize the prewar state governments and that the Confederates were to be given a general amnesty.

Considering Lincoln's overriding philosophy of wanting to ease the errant "sister" states back into the Union at the end of the Rebellion, Sherman's provisions seemed in accord. But it is doubtful that even Lincoln, had he lived, could have circumvented the radicals in his own government who were bent on revenge on the Southern states and their leaders who had started this most costly and horrible war.

It was on Lincoln's last full day at City Point, April 7, 1865, that he received the telegraphed message from Gen. Phil Sheridan, in charge of the cavalry in pursuit of Lee on his retreat toward Appomattox. It was originally sent to Grant, who was in the field yet was sending all dispatches on to Lincoln. "If the thing is pressed," read Sheridan's message,

"I think Lee will surrender." With typical brevity, Lincoln telegraphed one of his last orders to Grant: "Let the *thing* be pressed." A week and a day later, he would be dead.[1]

RICHMOND

SINCE IT WAS THE FOCAL POINT FOR SO many Federal campaigns as well as the symbol of Confederate power and center of Confederate government, Richmond, the capital of the southern Confederacy, is one of the most significant sites in American history.

Though Richmond has changed since the Civil War (and, in fact, was changed because of the fires set by retreating Confederates as the war was coming to a close), much of historic Richmond still remains. Richmond is truly a Renaissance city of the south. If Atlanta is the financial capital of the Deep South, then Richmond, with its banks, insurance companies, and brokerage houses, certainly is the financial capital of the Upper South.

In 1607, within a week of his landing at Jamestown, Capt. Christopher Newport sailed up the James to the falls near the site of present-day Richmond. A fort was established there two years later but was abandoned. By 1733 William Byrd II began to establish the cities of Richmond and Petersburg because they, "being the uppermost Landing of the James and Appomattox Rivers, are naturally in-

RICHMOND, VIRGINIA, IS reached from north or south by taking I-95 or from the east or west by taking I-64. Your first stop should be the National Park Service's Chimborazo Visitor Center, at 3215 East Broad Street (between 32nd and 35th streets). Heading south on I-95, take exit 10-A and turn east onto Franklin Street. Follow Franklin to 18th Street and turn left. Follow 18th to Broad Street and turn right. Proceed to Chimborazo Visitor Center. Heading north on I-95, take exit 10. Follow the road over the railroad and onto 17th Street. Follow 17th Street to Broad Street and turn left. Proceed to the Chimborazo Visitor Center.

The White House of the Confederacy is located at 12th and East Clay Streets; Tredegar Iron Works is located between the James River and the canal at the south end of 6th Street; Hollywood Cemetery is at Cherry and Albermarle Streets; Belle Isle sits in the middle of the *continued on page 141*

tended for Marts, where the Traffick of the Outer Inhabitants must Center." [2]

Through the colonial period Richmond grew slowly, but it was made capital of Virginia in 1779. Real growth came after the end of the Revolution. The development of Richmond as a center for transportation began with the opening of a canal from Richmond to Westham in 1790. In 1836 the Richmond, Fredericksburg, and Potomac Railroad roared out of the city at an astonishing ten miles per hour, scaring the wits out of its passengers. By 1840 the canal had stretched to Lynchburg, linking the Virginia Piedmont with the Virginia Tidewater and, coincidentally, to the rest of the world via the James River and the Chesapeake Bay.

By the 1840s Richmond had taken over from Williamsburg as the social center of Virginia, but political fires were smoldering beneath the fashionable exterior. In the spring of 1861, Virginia seceded from the Union; on May 29 the capital of the Confederacy was moved from Montgomery, Alabama, to Richmond, and the city became the target of Northern military aggression.

Life in Richmond in early 1861 was a series of balls and parties, teas, and sewing circles. But it wasn't long before the wounded from the battle at Manassas Junction began trickling, then flowing, into the city. Spring 1862 brought the war to the Richmonders'

continued from page 140
James and is located at the end of 7th Street; the site of Libby Prison is at 20th and Cary Streets; and Monument Avenue is an extension of W. Franklin Street.

doorsteps, as McClellan drove his army up the peninsula between the James and York rivers close enough to Richmond for his men to set their pocket watches by the chiming of the city's church bells. McClellan, however, was pushed back down the peninsula by Robert E. Lee during the Seven Days' Battles. The flow of wounded became a flood.

The spring of 1864 brought a more formidable Northern foe in the person of Gen. Ulysses S. Grant, who coordinated a drive against Lee's army that would eventually end the war. Since Lee was committed to protecting the capital of the Confederacy with his army, and Lee's Army of Northern Virginia was Grant's stated objective, Richmond necessarily became an integral part of Northern aims in the last year of the war. The wounded coming into Richmond then became a deluge of biblical proportions, and the evacuation of Richmond after Petersburg fell in 1865 a hegira worthy of the Exodus.

Lincoln visited Richmond after it fell on April 4, 1865. He rode the *River*

Queen up the James, transferred to the USS *Malvern*, and then was rowed on a gig to the shore near Rockett's Landing. In spite of being in a former enemy capital, Lincoln walked a good bit of the way surrounded by a crowd made up mostly of blacks, in awe and curious to finally see their emancipator. He visited the former residence of Jefferson Davis, the White House of the Confederacy, and toured the abandoned house with great interest. He was provided with a carriage and rode with his son and Adm. D. D. Porter as well as a captain on a tour of the captured capital of the Confederacy. ∎

☛ **W H A T · T O · S E E** A National Park Service driving tour that follows remnants of earthworks and battle sites for one hundred miles tells of the extent of the fighting for and defense of Richmond. A thorough tour of historic Richmond and the battlefields around the outskirts is always recommended.

Though a good bit of the city was burned by Confederates when they evacuated the city (and the section is still called the "burnt district"), many historic buildings remain and are in use. Several buildings and sites that are not associated with the James River are still essential to the story of Civil War Richmond.

The White House of the Confederacy, home of Confederate president Jefferson Davis and his family during the war, has recently been restored to its appearance when the Davises resided there. Many original Davis furnishings are on display. The large, new Museum of the Confederacy in the rear of the grounds houses thousands of historic artifacts of the Confederacy, including Robert E. Lee's sword, personal weapons, camp equipment, and the uniform he wore at the surrender at Appomattox. Military equipment belonging to Stonewall Jackson, Joseph E. Johnston, and Jeb Stuart are also displayed. The sword that Confederate general Lewis Armistead carried across the stone wall in Pickett's Charge at Gettysburg is on display. In storage are shelf upon shelf of original Confederate regimental battle flags, many captured during the war, others laid down regretfully and tearfully at the surrender ceremonies at Appomattox—a few still stained with the blood of martyrs to a misbegotten cause. And on the grounds outside rest an anchor and the drive shaft salvaged from the scuttled CSS *Virginia (Merrimack)*.

Chimborazo Park is the location of the Richmond National Battlefield

continued on page 143

continued from page 142
Park and the National Park Service Visitor Center. A tour of the battlefields around Richmond should begin here, where exhibits and audio-visual programs give some background and up-to-date maps and literature are available. The National Park Service Visitor Center is on the site of Chimborazo General Hospital, built in 1862 to treat eventually almost 76,000 sick and wounded soldiers of the Confederacy. Standing outside the Visitor Center and gazing across Chimborazo Park, it is almost impossible to imagine the suffering that occurred here, as shattered young men were brought here, died, or recovered to live with a missing limb or lingering effects of disease for the rest of their lives.

Tredegar Iron Works is the site of one of the largest, and certainly the most famous, munitions plants in the Confederacy. Iron plate armor for the warship *Virginia*, made famous by her clash with the USS *Monitor*, was rolled here as well as hundreds of cannons for the armies of the Confederacy.

Hollywood Cemetery can be considered the "National Cemetery of the Confederacy." The names on the headstones and monuments include Jeb Stuart, Jefferson Davis, George Pickett, and Douglas Southall Freeman. A visit to the section beneath the gigantic stone pyramid and a glance across the hundreds of headstones, many saying merely "unknown," in the section marked with a stone declaring "Gettysburg Dead" will help one understand why the name of the small Pennsylvania town is still very much like a curse in Virginia.

The prison of Belle Isle sits in the middle of the James River. At the beginning of the war, when prisoner exchanges were common, the prison conditions at Belle Isle were adequate. As the war continued and the exchange system was abandoned, Belle Isle, like most of the prisons in both the North and the South, grew overcrowded, holding anywhere from 6,000 to 10,000 Union prisoners and becoming one of the largest prisons in the Confederacy. Artillery was menacingly perched on the river bluffs overlooking Belle Isle, discouraging any attempts at escape.

Libby Prison was the former ship chandlery of Luther Libby, whose sign, "L. Libby & Son, Ship Chandlers," was linked with the prison his large, rented warehouse suddenly became when it was commandeered at the beginning of the war. Hence the name became synonymous with the horror and anguish

continued on page 144

continued from page 143

of cold, overcrowded, vermin-infested prisons of the Civil War. Libby Prison held only commissioned officers from the Union Army.

A drive along Monument Avenue is a history lesson in bronze. Statues of Robert E. Lee, Stonewall Jackson, Jeb Stuart, Jefferson Davis, and Commodore Matthew Fontaine Maury, the famous oceanographer, stand along the broad avenue.

The *Annabel Lee*, a replica paddlewheel three-decker riverboat, plies the James regularly spring, summer, and fall and is available for charters, including during the Christmas season. Heritage Cruise Line offers lunch, Sunday brunch, dinner, and moonlight party cruises downriver to Drewry's Bluff, about ten miles. Longer, three-hour "plantation" cruises, with brunch or dinner to Westover Plantation, are also available. If you want to see the river as the soldiers—and Abraham Lincoln—saw it and don't have your own boat, this is the way do it. Call (804) 222-5700 during regular working hours.

If you do have your own boat, a number of launch sites are accessible along the James, including one right across from where the *Annabel Lee* docks, as well as numerous ramps and marinas with overnight accommodations downriver.

Notes

1. Sheridan, 342.
2. *Virginia: A Guide to the Old Dominion*, 286.

CONCLUSION

IT'S EASY TO SAY, especially with hindsight, that the Confederates—because of their lack of manufacturing facilities, manpower, and modern machine technology—were a beaten nation in the American Civil War before the first shots were ever fired.

But other factors—some physical, some emotional, some even spiritual—affect wars and their outcomes. A Confederate victory in the Civil War was not dependent upon Southerners subjugating the Northern forces; it depended, at least in part, upon frustrating the Northern forces long enough that they would tire of attempting to subjugate the South.

How many more costly invasions of the South would the people of the North have tolerated? Lincoln was reelected once; would he have been reelected again in 1868 if the war had still been draining life out of the North at the enormous rate demanded by Grant's campaigns? Vietnam taught us how divisive a protracted war can be. The Civil War was divisive to begin with. If Grant had failed in his Virginia Campaign of 1864 and had been forced to turn back because he did not have the rivers for the massive resupply that was necessary, would the populace of the North have supported the loss of another 50,000 or more men in yet another campaign into the South in 1865? Or 1866? Or 1867?

It was to the South's advantage to prolong the war if they could. And control of the rivers was absolutely essential for the South to be able to do so.

Opening the rivers of Virginia—especially the James, with its numerous navigable tributaries—would have opened Virginia to the world. For example, after Charleston, South Carolina, was sealed off by Union forces, Wilmington, North Carolina, became a popular port on the East Coast for blockade runners. In 1864, quite late in the war and long after the "paper" blockade had supposedly become a real one,

168 blockade runners entered Wilmington, often at the rate of three or even four ships per day. That same year, 179 ships left Wilmington bound for Nassau, Bermuda, or Halifax, of which only fifteen were listed as being captured or destroyed by the Union blockade. North Carolina's wartime governor, Zebulon Vance, boasted that enough materials came into North Carolina to make uniforms for 125,000 soldiers, including 45,000 pairs of shoes and 36,000 to 50,000 blankets. Vance estimated North Carolina's profit during the war at $2,500,000 from importing and manufacturing goods. (Vance may have bragged a little too much on this point: Some state officials cut that figure in half.)[1]

If opening the rivers of Virginia to the world would have aided the Confederate cause there, denying their use to the Union would have led to even greater gains for the Confederacy, especially in the last crucial campaigns against the Army of Northern Virginia.

The Union Army under Grant was known for conspicuous consumption in both men and matériel. The operations of logistics at City Point were some of the most massive ever known in warfare to that time. The large Eppes Mansion on the bluff overlooking the confluence of the James and Appomattox rivers was taken over by the Quartermaster Corps. The commanding general had his headquarters in tents in the summer and in a small log cabin in the winter, no doubt indicative of both Grant's personal lack of ostentation and his realization of what—and who—really kept his army in the field. Fifteen hundred tons of supplies were off-loaded every day at City Point. How long would the Union Armies have been able to remain in the field without those supplies after winter set in? Robert E. Lee could have told Grant how long an army can fight with only the supplies it is able to carry.

Wagons and railroads could play only a secondary role in supplying Grant's armies in the field by getting the supplies from the ships to the armies. Railroads could have supplied nearly as much as ships, but wagon trains, never. An average wagon and team took up about forty feet of road plus about five feet between the team and the next wagon. Only about ten feet of that length—the wagon itself—was available for carrying supplies. At forty-five feet per wagon, only about 58 wagons would fit along a half mile of road. With the need for about 25 wagons per 1,000 men, the Union Army for the Battle of Gettysburg alone would have needed at least 2,425 wagons. End-to-end they would have taken up twenty-one miles or more of road. At the beginning of May 1864 the Army of the Potomac was supplied over winding wilderness roads by 4,000 wagons, and this was *after* paring down for the upcoming campaign. Lines that long are extremely vulnerable and therein lies the problem with wagon trains and railroads, even when used behind the lines.

A long, slow-moving wagon train of supplies was not only less efficient than a ship in terms of tons of supplies transported but also more vulnerable to everything from cavalry and artillery to mere citizenry with axes chopping out the spokes of the wheels, exactly what happened during Lee's retreat from Gettysburg. And it would have taken divisions of men to guard—from mounted men bent upon tearing up and destroying ties and rails—the hundreds of miles of railroad track needed to bring supplies from Washington to the theater of operations near Richmond.

A ship moving relatively swiftly through the water, however, was a difficult target. Artillerists were trained for and used to firing at other stationary guns in battery or at slow-moving lines of infantry. Ships presented the problem of a deflection shot, which was common to World War II gunners firing against airplanes but practically unknown to Civil War artillerists and virtually impossible to accomplish with the equipment they used. Additionally, ships drift from side to side even when moving forward, presenting an even tougher target. And most artillery was set up on bluffs overlooking the rivers. As the ships approached, the guns could no longer be depressed far enough to strike them. Land-based artillerists rarely, if ever, had the opportunity to practice-fire against real moving ships. Usually their first battle against ships was their only practice.

When ships and gunboats began being built with boilers below the waterline protected by coal storage bins outboard of them, they often took the hits of artillery with little damage. What a small band of mounted raiders could do to a wagon train or railroad, they normally could not do to a ship. Once the Union Army flanked and secured the larger forts overlooking the rivers, such as Fort Brady on the James or Yorktown and Gloucester Point on the York, their supplies could flow indefinitely.

More Confederate torpedoes (mines) in the rivers would have helped. About forty-three Union vessels ran into Confederate torpedoes throughout the waters of the Confederacy. Twenty-nine were sunk and another five were damaged seriously.[2] But even many Confederates were against this type of "barbaric" warfare, believing it uncivilized in the days when war had rules by which to fight. Probably the most important aspect of the use of torpedoes was their effect upon the morale of ships' commanders and crews. Once torpedoes were discovered in a channel, operations came to a virtual standstill until channel-clearing devices could be used.

What the South really needed was effective, organized river operations from her own navy to deny the use of the rivers to the Federals. But to have that, she also needed a coordinated effort from her armies to protect those ships and the land along the rivers. That fine-tuned, closed-loop coordination between army and navy, utilizing the ships on the rivers for supply of the armies, which in turn protected the ships and landings on the rivers, only happened during the Civil War with one army: the Union Army under Ulysses S. Grant.

Notes

1. Wise, 225, 233–50.
2. Perry, 199–201.

APPENDIX A:
Suggested Tours

To SEE AS many Civil War sites along the rivers as possible in the most convenient way, there are logical routes that you can follow. Although this guide is not meant to be a site-by-site tour book, my experience in finding and visiting these sites while researching—as well as getting lost along the way—has left me with some ideas for suggested tours. These tours can be segmented, combined, or expanded to suit available time and touring endurance.

THE UPPER POTOMAC RIVER

THE BEST WAY, but not necessarily the most convenient way, to see the Civil War sites on the upper Potomac is to bicycle along the Chesapeake & Ohio Canal towpath. Even a day trip of cycling several miles along the C & O Canal to visit just two or three sites is worth the time

Since not everyone is inclined to tour by bicycle, an automobile trip may be a preferable alternative. The sites on the upper Potomac are quite spread out, with some on the north side of the river and others on the south side. They really don't lend themselves to one contiguous automobile tour, but rather to three, starting at Williamsport, Shepherdstown, or Leesburg.

For a tour of the Potomac and C & O Canal crossings used by the Confederates in the Gettysburg Campaign, start at Williamsport, Maryland. Falling Waters can be seen from both sides of the Potomac, and McCoy's Ferry and Fort Frederick are also within short driving distances of Williamsport. Half a day, depending on the distance of your home from Williamsport, should be enough time to see these four sites.

Start at Shepherdstown, West Virginia, for a tour of Boteler's Ford on the C & O Canal, the Antietam Battlefield, and Harpers Ferry. Harpers Ferry can be reached by following signs from either Shepherdstown or Sharpsburg, Maryland, the location of the Antietam Battlefield. Allow a whole day to see Harpers Ferry, the Antietam Battlefield, and the sites between.

Leesburg, Virginia, is an excellent starting place for a tour of the Civil War sites in its area. The Ball's Bluff battlefield and National Cemetery are accessible by following signs from the Route 15 Leesburg bypass. At the bottom of Ball's Bluff, lying in the Potomac, is Harrison's Island. Return to the Route 15 bypass around Leesburg and follow it north. Cross the Potomac by ferry boat at White's Ferry, travel to White's Ford by following White's Ferry Road and turning left on Martinsburg Road to Dickerson Conservation Park. Retrace your route to White's Ferry and drive to Edward's Ferry by following River Road south. This tour should take about half a day.

THE LOWER POTOMAC RIVER

ALLOW A DAY to see Arlington, Alexandria, and Mount Vernon, all of which have guided tours available. A side trip south to Aquia Creek and Belle Plain is possible, but since both of these sites are closer to Fredericksburg, Virginia, you may want to include them in a tour of the Rappahannock River.

Fort Washington can be included in the day you spend visiting Arlington, Alexandria, and Mount Vernon, if you cross the Potomac via Route 495. Or, take a day or overnight trip to visit the sites from Fort Washington southward along Route 5 to Point Lookout.

THE RAPPAHANNOCK RIVER

A TOUR OF the sites along the Rappahannock River should start in the vicinity of Culpeper, Virginia. About eight miles east of Culpeper, just off Route 15, is Elkwood and Route 674, which takes you to the Kelly's Ford battle site. If you're coming from the north on Route 15, Elkwood is about 2.5 miles beyond the crossing of the Rappahannock. From Kelly's Ford, follow Route 620 to Route 3. Take

Route 3 toward Fredericksburg. About .75 miles from the intersection of Routes 620 and 3, where the road crosses the Rapidan, is the site of Germanna Ford. Follow Route 3 to the Chancellorsville Visitor Center, then take Route 610 heading northwest (a left turn at the end of Bullock Road on the Chancellorsville Tour Route) to Ely's Ford.

Return to the Chancellorsville Battlefield and follow Route 3 to Fredericksburg. You may even want to drive directly from Germanna Ford to the Fredericksburg Visitor Center and begin the tour of the four major battlefields around Fredericksburg from there. The National Park Service tour route begins at the Fredericksburg Visitor Center, and Ely's Ford can be a side trip from Chancellorsville.

The tour of the four battlefields around Fredericksburg—Chancellorsville, Spotsylvania, the Wilderness, and Fredericksburg—can be done in a day, but the city of Fredericksburg has its own guided tour and numerous Colonial and Revolutionary Period sites. Many fine restaurants and accommodations are available if you plan to stay overnight. While you are in the Fredericksburg area, you may want to make a short drive to Belle Plain on Potomac Creek and Aquia Creek.

From Fredericksburg, follow Route 17 southeast to Port Royal. Continue southeastward on Route 17 to Tappahannock, where you can take a commercial cruise of the Rappahannock. Route 17 will lead to Urbanna, and then south to Gloucester Point and Yorktown.

You may want to design your own tour depending on how much time you have to spend. Route 17 also leads to Newport News, Portsmouth, and the Norfolk area, mentioned later as a separate tour. From Route 17 at Yorktown you can reach the Colonial Parkway to Williamsburg, Jamestown, and the areas listed in the James River section.

THE YORK RIVER

A TOUR OF the sites on the York River can be combined with either a tour of the lower Rappahannock or a tour of the lower James. Williamsburg is a good place to start a tour of these areas, but a long day trip out of Fredericksburg can get you to Gloucester Point and Yorktown, and a swing toward Richmond will take you to the White House on the Pamunkey. Perhaps the best way to see the area of the White House on the Pamunkey is to include it as a side trip on the Richmond National Battlefield Park tour offered by the National Park Service.

THE JAMES RIVER

THE NUMEROUS SITES located along the James were often important in more than one campaign over the four years of Civil War. It is virtually impossible to set up a chronological tour that would not inconvenience someone. As with the upper Potomac, segmenting the various geographical areas along the Virginia Peninsula may be the best way to see the sites.

Perhaps the most logical way to tour the James is to start in Richmond and visit the Civil War battle sites as they are shown in the Richmond National Battlefield Park's tour map. This route circles clockwise to the northeast of Richmond. After Malvern Hill Battlefield the tour route strikes Route 5. A five-mile ride toward Richmond on Route 5 will take you to the battlefield park road leading to the Fort Harrison/Fort Brady complex.

After visiting Fort Brady, return to Kingsland Road. Kingsland Road will take you past Varina Road, from which the privately owned Aiken's Landing area can be approached, and Deep Bottom Road, which leads to Deep Bottom. Kingsland Road will also return you to Route 5. Turn right on Route 5 to get to Williamsburg.

Watch carefully on Route 5 for the signs to the various James River Plantations located along the route, including Shirley, Berkeley, Westover, and Evelynton.

Williamsburg, on Route 5, should be considered an overnight destination. In addition to its proximity to the Civil War sites along Route 5 and those on the Virginia Peninsula, Williamsburg is unique because of its restored Colonial appearance, costumed historical interpreters, fine food, and delightful shops. It is impossible to picture early Virginia history without an after-dinner, summer night's stroll along the darkened Duke of Gloucester Street or a visit to the formal gardens behind the main facades of the restored brick dwelling houses downtown. Be sure to take an eight-mile drive from Williamsburg along the Country Road to Carter's Grove, which has been restored as a living, eighteenth-century plantation and is the site of the seventeenth-century settlement of Wolstenholme Towne on the grounds at the river's edge.

After seeing everything in and around Williamsburg, your next destination should be Yorktown and its Revolutionary and Civil War sites. Take the Colonial Parkway, which is administered by the National Park Service, from Williamsburg to Yorktown and Gloucester Point. After visiting those sites you can continue down the peninsula to visit Norfolk and its surrounding cities. (See the Lower James River tour.)

If you do not travel to Norfolk, return to Williamsburg via the Colonial Parkway, then follow Route 31 to Jamestown—the site of the first permanent English settlement on the North American continent. Alternatively, follow the Colonial Parkway all the way to Jamestown

From Jamestown, watch for signs for Route 31 to take the Jamestown-Scotland Ferry across the James River, and then follow Route 31 to Route 10. Travel toward Hopewell on Route 10 and follow the signs to Flowerdew Hundred Plantation. Continue on Route 10 until you pick up the Richmond National Battlefield tour route, where Route 156 joins Route 10. Follow the tour route to visit City Point, Bermuda Hundred, and associated battlefields, as well as Fort Darling and Drewry's Bluff. Finally, Route 95 north, which you will see as you exit Drewry's Bluff, will return you to Richmond.

NORFOLK

The Norfolk area on the lower James has so much to see that it can't be included in a tour of the other sites on the Virginia Peninsula. Plan to spend at least a day at Norfolk, Portsmouth,

Newport News, Hampton, Fort Monroe, and Hampton Roads. Make it a destination, stay overnight, and experience the cruises, the seaside ambience, and the history of the numerous Civil War sites—as well as the pre- and post-Civil War attractions—so abundant near this world-famous seaport. You will enjoy the time spent in this part of Virginia.

APPENDIX B:
Visitors' Information

THE FOLLOWING IS a list of addresses and phone numbers for sources of pamphlets and information about historic places along the rivers.

THE UPPER POTOMAC RIVER

The Chesapeake & Ohio Canal
   National Historical Park
c/o Superintendent
Ferry Hill House
P.O. Box 4
Sharpsburg, MD 21782

Fort Frederick State Park
P.O. Box 1
11100 Fort Frederick Road
Big Pool, MD 21711
(301) 842-2155

THE LOWER POTOMAC RIVER

Arlington House
c/o Superintendent
G. Washington Memorial Parkway
Turkey Run Park
McLean, VA 22102

Mount Vernon Trail
c/o Superintendent
G. Washington Memorial Parkway
Turkey Run Park
McLean, VA 22101

Alexandria Convention &
   Visitors Bureau
221 King Street
Alexandria, VA 22314
(703) 838-4200

The Lee-Fendall House
614 Oronoco Street
Alexandria, VA 22314
(703) 548-1789

Robert E. Lee Boyhood Home
607 Oronoco Street
Alexandria, VA 22314
(703) 548-8454

Fort Washington
c/o Superintendent
National Capital Parks-East
1900 Anacostia Drive, SE
Washington, DC 20020

Historic Port Tobacco
c/o The Society for the Restoration
   of Port Tobacco
Port Tobacco, MD 20677

Charles County Historical Society
P.O. Box 261
Port Tobacco, MD 20677

Charles County Office of Tourism
Route 1, Box 1144
Port Tobacco, MD 20677

The Dr. Samuel A. Mudd House
  Museum
c/o The Dr. Samuel A. Mudd
  Society, Inc.
P.O. Box 1043
La Plata, MD 20646
(Special tours by appointment
  only.)
(301) 645-6870 or (301) 934-8464

Birthplace of Robert E. Lee
Stratford Hall Plantation
(Open 9:00 A.M. to 4:30 P.M. daily
  except Christmas.)
(804) 493-8038

Historic St. Mary's City
P.O. Box 39
St. Mary's City, MD 20686
(301) 862-0990

The Maryland Dove
c/o St. Mary's City Commission
P.O. Box 39
St. Mary's City, MD 20686
(301) 862-1666 or (301) 862-1634

St. Mary's County Historical
  Society
P.O. Box 212
Leonardtown, MD 20650

Chesapeake Bay Communications
1819 Bay Ridge Avenue
Annapolis, MD 21403
(301) 263-2662

Afro-American Heritage Museum
Highway 9 25N
Box 316
Waldorf, MD 20601

Calvert County Historical Society
P.O. Box 358
Prince Frederick, MD 20678

Calvert County Office of Tourism
Department of Economic
  Development
c/o Calvert County Courthouse
Prince Frederick, MD 20678

St. Clement's Island
Potomac River Museum, Inc.
Colton Point, MD 20626
(301) 769-2222

Point Lookout State Park
Star Route Box 48
Scotland, MD 20687

THE RAPPAHANNOCK RIVER

Fredericksburg and Spotsylvania
   National Military Park
c/o Superintendent
P.O. Box 679
Fredericksburg, VA 22404

Fredericksburg Visitor Center
Box FB
706 Caroline Street
Fredericksburg, VA 22401
(703) 373-1776

Urbanna Chamber of Commerce
Drawer C
Urbanna, VA 23175
(804) 758-5540

Rappahannock River Cruises
Warsaw, VA 22572
(May through October. Tours
   include a cruise to Tangier Island
   aboard the *Chesapeake Breeze*.)
(804) 333-4656

Rappahannock and Rapidan River
   Canoe Trips
Rappahannock Outdoor/
   Educational Center
3219 Fall Hill Avenue
Fredericksburg, VA 22401
(Trips past Kelly's Ford, Germanna
   Ford, and Ely's Ford.)
(703) 371-5085

THE YORK RIVER

York County Information Office
P.O. Box 532
Yorktown, VA 23690
(A walking tour of historic
   Yorktown is available.)
(804) 890-3300

Colonial National Historical Park
P.O. Box 210
Yorktown, VA 23690
(804) 898-3400

Yorktown Victory Center
P.O. Box 1776
Yorktown, VA 23690
(804) 887-1776

The Waterman's Museum
309 Water Street
Yorktown, VA 23690
(804) 887-2641

THE JAMES RIVER

Fort Monroe and the Casemate
   Museum
c/o The Casemate Museum
P.O. Box 341
Fort Monroe, VA 23651
(804) 727-3391

The Hampton Roads Naval
   Museum
1619 Dillingham Boulevard
Norfolk, VA 23411-3094
(804) 444-2243 or 444-8971

Norfolk Convention & Visitors
Bureau
236 East Plume Street
Norfolk, VA 23510
(800) 368-3097

Trolley Tours of Norfolk, the Naval
Base, Olde Towne Portsmouth,
and Oceana Air Station
P.O. Box 2096
Norfolk, VA 23501
(804) 623-3222

War Memorial Museum of Virginia
9285 Warwick Boulevard/
Huntington Park
Newport News, VA 23607
(804) 247-8523

Mariners Museum
Museum Drive
Newport News, VA 23606
(804) 595-0368

Evelynton Plantation
6701 John Tyler Highway
Charles City, VA 23030
(800) 473-5075

Berkeley Plantation
Route 5
Charles City, VA 23030
(804) 829-6018

Shirley Plantation
Route 2, Box 635
Charles City, VA 23030
(800) 232-1613

Chesterfield Historical Society
P.O. Box 40
Chesterfield, VA 23832
(Pamphlet on Bermuda Hundred
available. Call for price.)
(804) 748-1026

Flowerdew Hundred Foundation
1617 Flowerdew Hundred Road
Hopewell, VA 23860
(804) 541-8897 or (804) 541-8938

City Point Unit
c/o Superintendent
P.O. Box 549
Petersburg, VA 23804

Petersburg Information Services
P.O. Box 2107
Petersburg, VA 23804
(804) 861-8080

Richmond National Battlefield
Park
Chimborazo Visitor Center
3215 East Broad Street
Richmond, VA 23223

American Historical Foundation
Museum/U.S. Marine Raider
Museum
1142 West Grace Street
Richmond, VA 23220
(804) 353-1812

Black History Museum & Cultural
 Center of Virginia
00 Clay Street
Richmond, VA 23219
(804) 780-9093

MRCVB
East Marshall Street
Box C-250
Richmond, VA 23219
(Richmond visitor packets are
 available.)
(800) 365-7272

RIVER CRUISES
Hampton Visitor Center
710 Settlers Landing Road
Hampton, VA 23669
(*Miss Hampton II* Harbor Cruises,
 including Fort Monroe, Fort
 Wool, and Norfolk Naval Base.)
(804) 727-1102 or (804) 722-9102
In VA toll-free (800) 244-1040

Harbor Cruise, Inc.
530 12th Street
Newport News, VA 23607
(Newport News, Virginia, Harbor
 Cruises, including Newport
 News Shipyard and Norfolk
 Naval Base.)
(804) 245-1533

Heritage Cruises
P.O. Box 7735
Richmond, VA 23231
(Riverboat Cruises aboard the
 Annabel Lee, including the James
 below Richmond to Drewry's Bluff
 and the James River Plantations.)
(804) 222-5700

Tall Ship Cruises from Norfolk
P.O. Box 3125
Norfolk, VA 23514
(Sail aboard *American Rover*, a
 three-masted, topsail schooner.)
(804) 627-SAIL

Spirit of Norfolk Harbor Cruises
100 West Plume Street
Suite 116
Norfolk, VA 23510
(Cruise-ship experience, with
 entertainment.)
(804) 627-7771 or for groups,
 (804) 625-1748

Virginia's Harbor Tours on the
 Carrie B
End of Bay Street
Portsmouth, VA 23704
(A replica Mississippi River boat.
 Tours include Norfolk/
 Portsmouth Harbor. Leaves from
 Waterside in Norfolk or Portside
 in Portsmouth.)
(804) 393-4735

BIBLIOGRAPHY

ADC's *Chartbook of the Chesapeake Bay*. Alexandria, Va.: ADC of Alexandria, 1991.

Bay & River Guide to the Susquehanna and Chesapeake Bay and Its Tidal Tributaries. Virginia: Commonwealth of Virginia, 1989.

Chamberlain, Joshua L. *The Passing of the Armies*. Dayton: Morningside Bookshop, 1982.

Coddington, Edwin B. *The Gettysburg Campaign: A Study in Command*. New York: Charles Scribner's Sons, 1968.

Coggins, Jack. *Arms and Equipment of the Civil War*. 1962. Reprint. New York: The Fairfax Press, 1983.

Coski, John M. *The Army of the Potomac at Berkeley Plantation: The Harrison's Landing Occupation of 1862*. N.p., 1989.

Coulling, Mary P. *The Lee Girls*. Winston-Salem, N.C.: John F. Blair, Publisher, 1987.

Cowles, Capt. Calvin D., comp. *Atlas to Accompany the Official Records of the Union and Confederate Armies*. Washington, D.C.: Government Printing Office, 1891–1895.

Cullen, Joseph P. *The Peninsula Campaign 1862: McClellan & Lee Struggle for Richmond*. Harrisburg, Pa.: Stackpole Books, 1973; New York: Bonanza Books, n.d.

Davis, Burke. *Jeb Stuart: The Last Cavalier*. New York: The Fairfax Press, 1988.

Douglas, Henry Kyd. *I Rode with Stonewall*. Chapel Hill, N.C.: University of North Carolina Press, 1940; St. Simons Island, Ga.: Mockingbird Books, 1961.

Dowdey, Clifford. *Lee*. New York: Bonanza Books, 1965.

Flexner, James Thomas. *Washington: The Indispensable Man*. Boston: Little, Brown and Company, 1969; New York: The New American Library, 1984.

Frassanito, William A. *Grant and Lee: The Virginia Campaigns 1864–1865*. New York: Charles Scribner's Sons, 1983.

———. *Antietam: The Photographic Legacy of America's Bloodiest Day*. New York: Charles Scribner's Sons, 1978.

Freeman, Douglas Southall. *Lee's Lieutenants: A Study in Command*, 3 vols. New York: Charles Scribner's Sons, 1946.

Goertemiller, Richard, and Dixie Goertemiller, eds. *Guide to Cruising the Chesapeake Bay, 1990*. Annapolis, Md.: Chesapeake Bay Communications, 1989.

Grant, Ulysses S. *Personal Memoirs of Ulysses S. Grant*, 2 vols. New York: Charles L. Webster & Company, 1885; New York: Bonanza Books, n.d.

Hahn, Thomas F. *A Towpath Guide to the Chesapeake & Ohio Canal*. Shepherdstown, W.V.: The American Canal and Transportation Center, 1983.

Johnson, Robert Underwood, and Clarence Clough Buel, eds. *Battles and Leaders of the Civil War*, 4 vols. New York: Century Magazine, 1887; Secaucus, N.J.: Castle edition, n.d.

Kemmerle, Darlene. "3,384 Who Died." In *Oak Leaflets*. Maryland Forest, Park & Wildlife Service, n.p., n.d.

Long, E. B., and Barbara Long. *The Civil War Day by Day: An Almanac*. Garden City, N.J.: Doubleday & Co., 1971.

Luvaas, Jay, and Harold W. Nelson. *The U.S. Army War College Guide to the Battles of Chancellorsville & Fredericksburg*. Carlisle, Pa.: South Mountain Press, 1988; New York: Harper & Row Publishers, 1989.

Murfin, James V. *The Gleam of Bayonets: The Battle of Antietam and the Maryland Campaign of 1862*. New York: Thomas Yoseloff, 1965.

Nash, Howard P., Jr. *A Naval History of the Civil War*. Cranbury, N.J.: A. S. Barnes and Co., 1972.

Nesbitt, Mark. *35 Days to Gettysburg*. Harrisburg, Pa.: Stackpole Books, 1992.

1992 Virginia Travel Guide. Ardmore, Pa.: Independence Publishing, Inc., 1992.

Office of Publications Staff, National Park Service. *John Brown's Raid*. Washington, D.C.: U.S. Department of the Interior, 1973.

Perry, Milton F. *Infernal Machines: The Story of Confederate Submarine and Mine Warfare*. Baton Rouge, La.: Louisiana State University Press, 1965.

Porter, Horace. *Campaigning with Grant*. Bloomington, Ind.: Indiana University Press, 1961; New York: Bonanza Books, n.d.

Robertson, James I., Jr. *Civil War Sites in Virginia: A Tour Guide*. Charlottesville, Va.: University Press of Virginia, 1985.

Scheer, George F., and Hugh F. Rankin. *Rebels & Redcoats*. New York: The World Publishing Company, 1957; New York: New American Library, n.d.

Schildt, John W. *Stonewall Jackson: Day by Day*. Chewsville, Md.: Antietam Publications, n.d.

Sears, Stephen W. *George B. McClellan: The Young Napoleon*. New York: Ticknor & Fields, 1988.

Selby, John. *The Road to Yorktown*. New York: St. Martin's Press, 1976.

Sheridan, Philip. *Personal Memoirs of P. H. Sheridan*, 2 vols. New York: Charles L. Webster & Co., 1888.

Still, William N., Jr. *Iron Afloat: The Story of the Confederate Armorclads*. Nashville: Vanderbilt University Press, 1971.

Thomason, John. *Jeb Stuart*. New York: Charles Scribner's Sons, 1930.

Trudeau, Noah Andre. *Bloody Roads South: The Wilderness to Cold Harbor, May–June 1864*. Boston: Little, Brown and Company, 1989.

U.S. Navy Department. *Official Records of the Union and Confederate Navies in the War of the Rebellion*. Washington, D.C.: Government Printing Office, 1894–1922.

U.S. War Department. *War of the Rebellion: A Compilation of the Official Records of the Union and Confederate Armies*. 128 vols. Washington, D.C.: Government Printing Office, 1880–1901.

Wise, Stephen R. *Lifeline of the Confederacy: Blockade Running During the Civil War*. Columbia, S.C.: The University of South Carolina Press, 1988.

Writers' Program of the WPA in the State of Virginia, comp. *Virginia: A Guide to the Old Dominion*. New York: Oxford University Press, 1956.

INDEX

Aiken's Landing, 128–29
Alexandria, Virginia, 9, 35–36
Annabel Lee, 144
Antietam, battle of, 18, 21
Antietam Campaign, 1–2, 24
Antietam Creek, 10
Antietam National Battlefield, 19–20
Aquia Creek, Virginia, 10, 38–39
Arlington, Virginia, 9, 33–35
Arlington House, 34, 35
Arlington National Cemetery, 34
Armistead, Louis, 41–43
Armistead, Walker K., 41
Army Fifth Corps (Union), 53
Army of Northern Virginia (Confederate),
    15, 16, 21, 110
Army of the James (Union), 107–8
Army of the Potomac (Union), 9, 52–53
Averill, General (Union), 51

Baker, Edward, 28, 29
Ball's Bluff, 27–29
Barnes, James, 80–81
Battery Dantzler, 132
Battlefields, touring, 3–6
Battle of Antietam, 18, 21
Battle of Darbytown, 127
Battle of Drewry's Bluff, 94–95
Battle of Fort Stevens, 110
Battle of Fredericksburg, 54–59
    map, 56–57
Battle of Gettysburg, 15
Battle of Manassas Junction. *See* Bull Run
Battle of the Ironclads, 82–86
Beauregard, P. G. T., 109, 111, 112
Belle Isle, 140–41
    prison of, 143
Belle Plain, 39–41
Berkeley, William, Sir, 65
Berkeley Plantation, 98, 99, 101, 102–3
Bermuda Hundred, 109–12, 125
Bernard, Simon, 79
Big Bethel, 77
Birney, General (Union), 129
Blackford's Ford. *See* Boteler's Ford

Booth, John Wilkes, 44, 60
Boteler's Ford, 20, 21
Brady, Mathew, 41
Brompton Mansion, 58
Brown, John, 17–18, 22–23
"Bull Ring," 121
Bull Run, 10, 27
Burnside, Ambrose, 38, 54, 59, 128
Butler, Benjamin F., 82, 107–9, 109–11, 113,
    125, 132–33
Butterfield, Daniel, 100
Byrd, William, II, 140

Campbell, John, 123
Camp Hoffman, 45
Casemate Museum, 81
Cedar Run, 10
Chancellorsville Campaign, 53
Chatham Mansion, 58
Chesapeake & Ohio Canal, 10, 11–12
Chickahominy River, 72
Chimborazo General Hospital, 143
Chimborazo Park, 142–43
City Point, 113, 119–24
City Point Railroad, 120
Civil War battlefields, touring, 3–6
Cold Harbor, 112
Comstock, Colonel (Union), 113–14
Comstock, Lieutenant (Union), 68
Confederate Army, factors concerning,
    145–46
Confederate Cemetery, 58
Congress, USS, 82, 83
Conrad's Ferry, 28
Corbett, Boston, 60
Cornwallis, Earl Lord, 65–67
Cornwallis's Cave, 70
Crawford, William, 89
Culp, Wesley, 18–19
Cumberland, USS, 82, 83
Cumberland Valley Railroad bridge, 24–25
Custis, Martha. *See* Washington, Martha
    Custis
Custis, Mary Anne Randolph. *See* Lee,
    Mary Anne Randolph Custis

Dailey, John T., 51
Darbytown, battle of, 127
Davis, Jefferson, 81, 142, 143
Deep Bottom, 125–28
Depot Field Hospital, 121
de Rochambeau, Count, 66
Douglas, Henry Kyd, 17, 18, 19
Drewry, Augustus, 94
Drewry's Bluff, 94–95, 109
Dutch Gap Canal, 133

Early, Jubal, 30
Edward's Ferry, 28, 30–31
18th Mississippi Infantry (Confederate), 57
89th New York Infantry (Union), 58
Eisenhower, Dwight D., 92
Ellsworth, Elmer, 9
Ely's Ford, 53–54
Evans, Nathan G., 28
Evelynton Plantation, 102
Ewell, Richard S., 121

Falling Waters, 15–16
The Farmer's Register, 102
Federal James River gunboat flotilla
    (Union), 78
Ferry Hill plantation, 17
1st Connecticut Heavy Artillery
    (Union), 131
Flowerdew Hundred Plantation, 115–18
Fort Brady, 131–32
Fort Darling, 95
Fort Foote, 43
Fort Frederick, 12
Fort Harrison, 129–30
Fort Monroe, 3, 68, 77, 79–82
Fort Stevens, 109, 111
    battle of, 110
Fort Warburton, 41
Fort Washington, 41–43
Fort Wool, 79
Frassanito, William, 40, 133
Fredericksburg, CSS, 134
Fredericksburg
    battle of, 54–59
    1862, 54–59
Fredericksburg and Potomac Railroad, 38
Fredericksburg Campaign, 53
Freeman, Douglas Southall, 4

Galena, USS, 94
Gardner, James, 41
Garrett farmhouse, 60
Germanna Ford, 52–53

Gettysburg, battle of, 15
Gettysburg Campaign, 1–2, 16
Gloucester Point, 65–67
Goldsborough, Louis M., 93
Gosport Navy Yard, 81, 87, 88, 89, 93
Graham, C. K., 110
Grant, Ulysses S., 3, 38, 39, 49, 53, 60,
    74–75, 78, 103, 107–9, 110, 112,
    117–18, 119, 122, 124, 125, 126–27,
    129–30, 132, 134–36, 139, 141
    crosses the James, 113–14
Guadeloupe, HMS, 66
Guide to Cruising Chesapeake Bay, 47

Hahan, Thomas F., 21
Halleck, Major General (Union), 113
Hampton Roads, 77, 78, 82–86
Hampton Roads Naval Museum, 88
Hamtramck Guards, 18–19
Hancock, Winfield Scott, 53, 114, 125,
    127, 128
Harpers Ferry, 10, 14, 22–23
Harrison, Benjamin, V, 98
Harrison, William Henry, 98
Harrison's Island, 29
Harrison's Landing, 97, 98–103
Hill, A. P., 20
Hill, Daniel Harvey, 55, 59
Hollywood Cemetery, 140, 143
Howlett Line, 132
Huger, Benjamin, 80, 81
Hunter, Robert, 123

I Rode with Stonewall (Douglas), 18
*Iron Afloat: The Story of the Confederate
    Armorclads* (Still), 136
Ironclads, battle of the, 82–86

Jackson, James, 9
Jackson, Thomas J. (Stonewall), 14, 19, 23
James River, 1, 2, 3,
    1862, 77–78
    1864, 107–9
    Grant crosses the, 113–14
    information sources concerning, 157–59
    map of, 76, 106
    plantations, 96
    suggested tours of, 152–54
    traveling the, 103–5
James River Squadron (Confederate), 131
Johnston, Joseph E., 61, 62, 69, 72–73, 80,
    81, 139
Jones, General (Grumble), 26

Kelly's Ford, 50–52
Kershaw, Joseph B., 121
King, W. R., 128
Kiser, Taft, 118

LaFayette, Marquis de, 66
Lee, Arthur, 62
Lee, Charlotte Wickham, 74
Lee, George Washington Custis, 79, 121
Lee, Mary Anne Randolph Custis, 33, 72, 79
Lee, Robert E., 1–2, 15, 16, 19, 21, 22, 23,
    24, 33–34, 50, 55, 58, 69, 72–73, 79–81,
    97, 100–1, 110, 112, 127, 130, 141
Lee, William Henry Fitzhugh (Rooney),
    25–26, 72, 73, 74
L'Enfant, Pierre, 41
Lexington Park, 44
Libby Prison, 141, 143–44
Lincoln, Abraham, 13, 61, 62, 93, 122, 123,
    124, 126, 139–40, 141–42

McClellan, George B., 3, 13, 19, 28, 61–63,
    68–69, 72–73, 78, 91–93, 97, 99–100,
    102, 141
McCoy's Ferry, 13
Magruder, John B., 68, 90
Mahone, William, 94
Malvern, USS, 142
Manassas Junction, battle of. See Bull Run
Mariner's Museum, 91
Marshall House, 36
Mary Martin, 124
Mathias Point, 10
Meade, George G., 15–16, 125
Meigs, Montgomery, 35
Merrimack, USS. See Virginia, CSS
Minnesota, USS, 82
Monitor, USS, 1, 77–78, 84–86, 92, 94
Moore House, 70
Mount Vernon, 36–38
Mount Vernon Ladies Association, 38
Mudd, Samuel, 44
Museum of the Confederacy, 142

Nelson House, 70
Newport, Christopher, 140
Newport News, Virginia, 90–91
Newport News Park, 91
Norfolk, Virginia, 86–88
    trolley tours of, 87–88

Oak Grove, battle at, 97
Occoquan, 10
Old Court House, 62

Old Point Comfort Lighthouse, 81
118th Pennsylvania (Union), 21
Onondaga, USS, 134–36
Ord, General (Union), 129

Packhorse. See Boteler's Ford
Pamunkey River, White House on, 71–75
Parker, William A., 134, 136
Peirsey, Abraham, 115
Pelham, John, 25, 50–52, 99
Peninsula Campaign
    June to August 1862, 97
    March to May 1862, 91–94
Pettigrew, General (Confederate), 16
Plantations, on the James River, 96
Point Lookout, Maryland, 43–45
Point of Rocks, 28
Pontoon bridge, 117–18
Pontoon crossing sites, 54–55
    upper and middle, 58
Porter, David, 139, 142
Porter, Horace, 113–14, 117, 122, 128, 129,
    130, 133, 134, 135
Port Royal, 59–60
Portsmouth, Virginia, 89–90
Portsmouth Lightship Museum, 89
Portsmouth Naval Shipyard Museum, 89
Port Tobacco, 44
Port Walthall Junction, 110
Potomac River, 1, 2
    cruising the, 45–47
    information sources concerning, 155–56
    lower, 32, 33
    suggested tours of, 149–50
    upper, 8, 9–10
Prince, Gene, 118
Punch Bowl, 40, 41

Rapidan River
    Ely's Ford on the, 53–54
    Germanna Ford on the, 52–53
Rappahannock River, 1, 2, 49–50
    information sources concerning, 157
    map of, 48
    suggested tours of, 150–51
Richmond, CSS, 134
Richmond, Virginia, 140–44
    map of, 138
Richmond National Battlefield Park, 71
River cruises, information sources
    concerning, 159
River Queen, 123, 124, 139, 141–42
Robert Gilchrist House, 60
Ruffin, Edmund, 102

St. Clements Island, 44
St. Mary's City, 44
St. Michaels, Maryland. *See* Point Lookout, Maryland
Second Corps of the Union Army, 53
Seven Days' Battles, 3, 69–71, 73, 97, 141
Seven Pines, 72, 97
17th Mississippi Infantry (Confederate), 57
7th Michigan Infantry (Union), 58
Seward, William H., Secretary of State, 123
Shackleford, Bessie, 50
Sharpe, George (Union), 122
Sharpsburg, Maryland, 19–20
Shenandoah River, 10
Shenandoah Valley, 2
Shepherdstown, 17–19, 28, *see also* Boteler's Ford
Sheridan, Philip, 127, 139
Sherman, William P. (Union), 139
Shirley Plantation, 101
Slave Auction Block, 58
Smith, William F., 110, 111
Stephens, Alexander, 123, 124
Still, William N., Jr., 136
Stone, Charles P., 28, 29
Stonewall Brigade, 19
Strode's Mill, 51
Stuart, James Ewell Brown (Jeb), 13, 15, 22, 23, 24, 26, 50, 51, 73, 98, 99
Swan Tavern Group, 70
Swift Creek, 110

3rd Indiana Cavalry (Union), 52
3rd Virginia Cavalry (Confederate), 51
13th Mississippi Infantry (Confederate), 57
35th Virginia Cavalry Battalion (Confederate), 26
Tindall, Robert, 65
Tindall's Point, 65
Tobacco Warehouse, 62
Tredegar Iron Works, 140, 143
Trent's Reach, 132–33
Trip-wire defenses, 111–12
Trolley Tours of Norfolk, 87–88

U.S. Christian Commission, 120
Union Army, factors concerning, 146–48
Union cause, importance of rivers to the, 1, 3
Urbanna, 1862, 61–63

"The Urbanna Plan," 61

Vance, Zebulon, 146
Varina. *See* Aiken's Landing
Virginia, CSS, 82–83, 84, 85–86, 91, 92, 93–94, 142, 143
Virginia Campaign, 38
Virginia massacre, 115
Virginia II, CSS, 134

"Walking Tour Guide of Old Town" (brochure), 36
War Memorial Museum of Virginia, 90
Warrior, HMS, 83
Warwick River, 68
Washington, Augustine, 36
Washington, George, 11, 36, 37–38, 41, 66, 71
Washington, John, 36
Washington, Lawrence, 37
Washington, Martha Custis, 71
Washington Artillery, 94
Watermen's Museum, 70
Waugh Point. *See* Belle Plain
Wayne, Anthony, 66
Weitzel, Godfrey, 111, 118
Westover Plantation, 101–3
Weyanoke Point, 118
White, E. V., 26
White, General (Union), 23
White, James. *See* White House (on the Pamunkey), 71–75
White House (on the Pamunkey), 71–75
White House Landing, 1864, 74–75
White House of the Confederacy, 140, 142
White's Ferry, 26
White's Ford, 24–26
Wilcox's Landing, 113, 114, 116
Willcox, John Vaughan, 116
Williamsport, Maryland, 14
Wilmington, North Carolina, 145–46
Windmill Point, 114
Woolridge Hill, 111
Worden, John L., 85

Yeardley, George, Sir, 115
York River, 1, 2, 3
    information sources concerning, 157
    map of, 64
    suggested tours of, 151–52
Yorktown, Virginia, 68–71
Yorktown Victory Center, 70